GOING HOME

IRISH STORIES
FROM THE EDGE OF DEATH

COLM KEANE

CAPEL
ISLAND

First published in Ireland in 2009

by

CAPEL ISLAND PRESS
36 Raheen Park, Bray,
County Wicklow, Ireland

ISBN 978-0-9559133-1-0

Printed by ColourBooks Ltd, Dublin
Typesetting and cover design by Typeform Ltd

For Seán

COLM KEANE has published 18 books including the number one bestsellers *Padre Pio: The Irish Connection* and *Nervous Breakdown*. He is a graduate of Trinity College, Dublin, and Georgetown University, Washington DC. As a broadcaster, he won a Jacob's Award and a Glaxo Fellowship for European Science Writers. His eight chart bestsellers include *The Jobs Crisis*, *Death and Dying* and *The Stress File*.

CONTENTS

There are more things in heaven and earth, Horatio, than are dreamt of in your philosophy.

Hamlet, Act 1, Scene V, William Shakespeare

INTRODUCTION

This book contains the most vivid descriptions ever provided by Irish people about what happens at the point of death. Some of those interviewed here have died. Fortunately, through the use of modern-day resuscitation techniques they have been restored to life. On their return from the gates of heaven they have recounted remarkable stories.

Many have gone through dark tunnels, entered an intense brightness, been welcomed by deceased family and friends, and encountered a 'superior being'. The vast majority say they felt calm and serene as they drifted away from their bodies to life on the other side. Virtually all have been marked forever by their extraordinary experiences.

For tens of thousands of years mankind has wondered about where we go when we die. All civilisations and cultures have tackled the issue. Even our Neanderthal ancestors, some 50,000 years ago, buried their deceased with food and stone implements to accompany them on their journeys from the land of the living to the land of the dead.

Since then many religions have dealt with the subject. Most have concluded that life continues after bodily death. Some promise eternal life in paradise. Others offer cycles of rebirth and reincarnation. However, despite appealing to trust, faith and belief, they have been remiss at establishing what really happens when we die.

Medicine hasn't helped either, espousing a clinical cycle of birth, ageing, disease, death and decay that is cold and misleading. Death, doctors tell us, occurs when the brain stops functioning. Our bodies – just like machines – shut down. Nothingness follows and we crumble to dust.

That premise, as this book shows, would appear to be well short of the mark. If the testimony in this book is to be believed – and it is both credible and reliable – then what awaits us after death stretches well beyond that moment when our vital bodily functions finally cease to work.

The origins of this book date back to September 1990, when an account of a remarkable near-death experience appeared in the local press. Most of the typical elements were there – the out-of-body travel, the tunnel, the sense of peace, the bright light, the welcoming by relatives, the encountering of a border or boundary, and the eventual return to real life.

Having stored the page in a file, I found myself coming back to it time and again over the years. It held a strange fascination, an unusual attraction, a compelling interest and appeal. In 2007 I eventually re-opened the file and resurrected the report. It led me, over the following years, to a nationwide search for other stories.

It wasn't an easy task. There were no dedicated research archives in Ireland and no significant coverage of the topic in the local or national press. Church sources, in particular, were less than helpful, arguing that what happens after death is a 'mystery' and advising me to leave it at that.

Some of those I contacted misunderstood the nature of the project, confusing it with a study of ghosts or the occult. Those of a religious persuasion were worried about a potential conflict with the tenets of their faith.

Many were nervous of being named and fearful of being categorised as strange, weird or unstable. Others struggled to describe the indescribable – happenings belonging to another dimension that involve intense feelings and sensations outside our normal linguistic range.

Yet the stories were there – and there in abundance. I was genuinely surprised by the huge number of ordinary people, living normal lives, who had extraordinary stories to tell. They related their anecdotes with remarkable clarity and consistency, and the details never changed when rechecked.

Above all, the interviewees in this book are solid, level-headed and sound. All are genuine and sincere. What follows are their honest accounts, in their own words, of their acquaintance with death. For all of us, this may be the nearest we will get to understanding where we go when we die.

Colm Keane

DISCOVERING THE LIGHT

Michael Paterson's heart stopped beating on Monday 28 September 1981. It was somewhere between late morning and early evening when he died. His body, at the time, was lying on an operating table in Belfast, surrounded by doctors battling to save his life. His physical form lay on the table but he was elsewhere. 'I was suddenly aware of being in a dark tunnel, with a light at the end of it,' he recalls. 'I was moving towards it.'

He felt calm and at peace as he drifted along. The light ahead was luminous, intense. 'It was like a circle of light which got bigger as I got closer. I was moving along in the blackness and the next thing I was in the light itself.' There he was surrounded by welcoming figures: 'It felt like these were friends or relatives but who they were I didn't know. I felt very comfortable. It was extremely pleasant.'

Back in the hospital the doctors fought to revive Michael's body which was in a very bad way. He had suffered severe physical injuries in a terrorist attack. He was badly smashed up. He had lost lots of blood. In sharp contrast to his body, the 'other' Michael was in a place where everything was tranquil and serene. 'It was like a spiritual experience,' he reflects. 'I felt very much at peace and felt very welcome.'

He also felt, however, that the time wasn't right. Aged 24, he was young, physically fit, just married: 'I got a sense of, "I don't belong here yet."' Almost immediately Michael returned to his body. 'It was,' he says, 'like a sudden return.' Eventually he learned that he had died briefly while in surgery. He learned, too, that what he had gone through on that day back in 1981 was a classic example of a near-death experience.

A near-death experience describes a range of extraordinary occurrences that can happen at the point of death. To begin with, those who are dying, or have clinically died, leave their physical body and float away. The vast majority feel serene and at peace despite the trauma they have gone through. A sense of calmness overwhelms them. They feel warm and happy.

Many enter a long dark tunnel with a bright, intense light at the end. They may travel along the tunnel and enter the light which, although very strong, isn't dazzling. The place they come to sometimes features lush countryside, green pastures, rich meadows and an abundance of flowers. They feel they are 'going home'. Familiar people, most likely deceased family members or former friends, often come to greet them. They may also meet a 'superior being', frequently believed to be God, who is compassionate and kind.

Many encounter a barrier, border or boundary. It may be a bridge, river or lake. Some undergo a life review, with images from their past lives flashing before their eyes. A decision then faces them – should they return or press on? Sometimes those they meet encourage them to 'go back', that 'it's not their time.' Other times they themselves reluctantly decide to return, despite feeling an overwhelming desire to cross over.

The journey back is quicker, almost instantaneous. Often on re-entering their bodies they feel disappointed and regretful about the choice they made. Many no longer fear dying. These features, as you might expect, vary in detail from person to person although many are commonly shared. Either way their lives on their return are dramatically changed, and memories of what they experienced remain for as long as they live.

Jimmy, from County Wexford, had a near-death experience when in his 50s. A long-time sufferer from heart trouble, he clinically died for 22 seconds following a series of cardiac arrests. 'I walked through the tunnel and stood in the light,' he recalls. 'I was in a lovely meadow which had flowers from every land, including exotic flowers. I walked a few yards and was standing on the edge of a river.

'There, on the opposite side of the river, I saw my sister who died when she was 16 years old. She was standing hand-in-hand with my father-in-law who had died. The two of them never knew each other. They beckoned me to come across. I had the feeling I was going into a new life. I went into the water and started to swim. When I was in the middle of the river they let their hands go and parted.

'Behind them was a light – a light of warmness, confidence and trust. There was someone standing in the light. I could see a form. The light seemed to come from two hands – like a statue of Jesus. No words can describe what I saw. This figure with outstretched hands came nearer and nearer. I wanted to catch those hands but could not swim any quicker.

'There was this feeling of being welcomed home. It got more intense as I got nearer. I put up my hands to touch the form with outstretched hands. But when just a finger-length from touching the hands I started to go backwards and the light went backwards. I came back to life again. I was disgusted when I came back. I wanted to stay there.'

For Jimmy, the experience was very gratifying: 'Standing there in the light, I knew I had made it. I was free of all pain and hospitals. It was a joyous feeling.' Others interviewed for this book echo his views. Jane Smyth, from County Wicklow, says: 'I was in a place that was magnificent. It had a little stream in the middle and green grass on both sides of the stream. It wasn't a huge river or anything. It was lovely. The peace was wonderful.'

Sarah, from County Donegal, felt at home with the people she met: 'I wanted to go to them as if they were long-lost relatives or ancestors or friends. It was an overwhelming desire.' Monica, from County Limerick, was similarly overjoyed: 'The experience has changed my life. When I am near a person that is dying now, I almost envy the beautiful experience that is awaiting them. I never cry for a person that is dead. It's a new beginning and they wouldn't want to return.'

As we have seen, one of the first steps in a near-death experience is for a person to drift out of their body before travelling away. Some combination of the tunnel travel, bright light, life review, greeting by relatives and meeting with a 'superior being' then takes place. However, it is also possible for someone to just leave their body and the other features never occur. The person, in other words, has a straightforward out-of-body experience.

Typically, a person may float away from their body and observe themselves down below. They might, for example, be watching themselves lying on an operating table or unconscious at the scene of a crash. Alternatively, they might travel long distances to faraway places. They eventually return to their body. These out-of-body journeys, although equally intriguing, are therefore more limited and restricted in scope than a near-death experience. They are also less intense.

Elizabeth, from County Down, had a classic out-of-body experience which occurred one night in bed. 'I felt I was leaving my body completely and moving off,' she recalls. 'I was floating up above myself. I could see myself clearly below but I knew the real me was the one above and it was just a body down below, just packaging. I thought, "This is weird. I don't like this. I'm going to die. I'm about to go."'

Kristian, from County Donegal, had an altogether stranger experience following a stabbing. 'I have a memory, when I was out cold in hospital, of being at the edge of a cliff, kind of hovering over the edge of it,' he recollects. 'It was night-time and it was dark. There was water maybe 50 metres down. The cliff went vertically down and the waves were crashing up against the bottom.

'I didn't have any thoughts. It was just nothingness, nothing going through my head. I felt myself being elevated up towards the sky. I hovered up about ten feet and then, suddenly, I felt myself coming back down again. It ended with me waking up about five or six hours later in Intensive Care.'

An estimated one in ten people have an out-of-body experience, representing some 600,000 Irish men, women and children. The incidence of near-death experiences is understandably lower although still substantial. A Gallup poll conducted in the USA established that one in every 20 Americans experience them. Applying this ratio to Ireland, the figure amounts to some 300,000 people.

For most, the near-death experience is overwhelmingly positive. There are, however, exceptions, with a small number of people having 'hellish' ones. Estimates vary. One study puts the figure for negative experiences as low as one in 100. At the upper limit it may be around one in six, seven or eight. Some out-of-body journeys can also be frightening, as we shall see later on in the book.

Anyone can have one or both, including males and females, and incorporating all cultures, races and creeds. Christians, Buddhists and Hindus have them. Atheists have them as well. All social classes and occupations are accounted for. Nor is the nature or cause of illness a barrier to inclusion. Whether the illness is prolonged or brief, following from an accident or chronic sickness, or resulting from a failed suicide attempt, it doesn't matter – the possibility of having a near-death or out-of-body experience is common to all.

Children have them too. Paediatrician Dr. Melvin Morse, who studied childhood cases for his book *Closer To The Light*, estimates that 70 per cent of children who face death have a near-death experience. According to another study, undertaken by the well-known researcher P. M. H. Atwater, only a tiny minority of children – three per cent – have a bad experience.

Children sometimes have their experiences following a near-drowning or high fever. Both can bring them to the edge of death. Following revival in the case of the near-drowning or recovery from the fever, they may eventually speak about what occurred. Unlike adults, they are generally willing to talk freely. Their testimony is also highly reliable because of their openness and innocence.

Among the childhood cases featured in this book is the story of singer Mickey Harte, from County Donegal, who fell into a stream as a kid and travelled out of his body. 'I remember seeing myself lying down below,' he recalls. 'I could see myself from above. I was just hovering there, watching myself. You'd wonder how as a child you could see yourself down there in that position. You'd wonder how you could even think of that as a kid, how you could conceptualise it.'

Another case concerns a four-year-old girl named Chris, from County Wicklow, who left her body while gravely ill. 'I was gone from the bed and was sitting on the window-ledge,' she remembers. 'I am 100 per cent sure I had died. I was out of my body, over by the window, although I could still see my body in the bed. I don't really know what happened. I was just in bed one minute and the next minute out of the bed.'

Many internationally-known names have also had near-death or out-of-body experiences. Actor Peter Sellers, famous for his *Pink Panther* films, witnessed the light following a heart attack in 1964. 'I felt myself leave my body,' he recalled. 'I just floated out of my physical form and I saw them cart my body away to the hospital.' Sellers died. 'I looked around myself and I saw an incredibly beautiful, bright, loving white light above me,' he said. 'I wanted to go to that white light more than anything.

'I knew there was love, real love, on the other side of the light which was attracting me so much. It was kind and loving and I remember thinking, "That's God." Then I saw a hand reach through the light. I tried to touch it, to grab onto it, to clasp it so it could sweep me up and pull me through it.' Instead, Sellers was told: 'It's not time. Go back and finish. It's not time.' He returned to his body, bitterly disappointed.

Actress Sharon Stone, of *Basic Instinct* fame, experienced something similar while fighting for her life in hospital in 2001. Stone almost died having haemorrhaged from a torn artery at the base of her skull. 'This brilliant, bright, white vortex of light was upon me. It was beautiful and very illuminating,' she said. 'Then I was met by some of my friends, people who are very dear to me. But it was over very fast and suddenly I was back in the room and in my own body. I came back from the abyss and I survived.'

Another great movie legend, Elizabeth Taylor, died for five minutes while undergoing surgery in the late 1950s. 'I was pronounced dead,' the star of *Cleopatra* recalled, 'and actually saw the light.' During the experience she was met by her former husband Mike Todd, who had died in a plane crash. 'I went to that tunnel, saw the white light, and Mike,' she explained. 'I said, "Oh, Mike, you're where I want to be." He said, "No. You have to turn around and go back because

11

there is something very important for you to do. You cannot give up now.'''

Yet another film star, Jane Seymour, who featured as a Bond girl in *Live And Let Die*, had an out-of-body experience back in the late 1980s. It followed an allergic reaction to penicillin, resulting in her dying for about 30 seconds. 'I literally left my body,' she explained. 'I saw the white light and I saw, from the corner of the room, them trying to resuscitate me and I saw a syringe with blood in it. I was above them, in the corner of the room, looking down. I remember my whole life flashing before my eyes.' Fortunately, Seymour returned to her body and lived.

Similar stories can be found in ancient texts. The Greek philosopher Plato, who lived from about 427–347 BC, chronicled one of the very first examples of a near-death experience. Although written long ago – well before the time of Christ – the details are remarkably familiar. The account relates the story of Er, a soldier who was killed in battle. Twelve days after his death he revived while on his funeral pyre and told of a remarkable journey to the other side.

He described how 'his soul left the body' and travelled towards a light which he said resembled a 'rainbow, but brighter and purer.' Accompanied by others who had died, he arrived at a place where there were entrances to both heaven and hell. Judges stood there deciding who was to turn right into heaven or left into hell. In Er's case, he was instructed that it was not yet his time but to return to his body. He was also told to inform others, back on earth, of the otherworld and what determines their fate.

Near-death experiences can also be found in ancient Irish manuscripts, where similarities with modern-day accounts are startling. In the old texts, brightness is everywhere. Scenes of glorious light are described. Bridges are crossed, which separate either heaven from hell or life from death. The bridges usually span rivers, valleys or lakes. Heaven, we are told, is a rich and wonderful place, always pleasant and with fertile land. Gardens and fields overflow with beautiful flowers. Sweet smells are everywhere.

People, often dressed in white, are welcoming and joyful. All is relaxed, peaceful and calm, with the only sounds coming from a low hum of voices or heavenly choirs. We are also informed, in many of these documents, how the soul travels towards the otherworld before turning back, indicating that the phenomenon of a near-death experience was well-known to Irish men and women since early times.

Perhaps the earliest Irish example of a near-death experience can be found in the story of Saint Fursa, who lived in the seventh century. In 633 he fell ill and appeared to have died. Plans were set in train to bury him. Ancient documents written within a century of his death describe how, instead of dying, his soul left his body and travelled to the other side. There he reputedly saw angelic choirs, witnessed heavenly singing and observed the great joys of the blessed.

People he recognised – holy men and priests from Ireland – greeted him and offered advice. He was also given a glimpse of the fires of hell. He described how devils flew through the flames, tormenting sinners. He received burns on his shoulder and jaw, which remained with him for the rest of his life. Eventually, we are informed, the soul of Fursa 'was restored to his body.' Inspired by the experience, he continued his missionary work in England and in France. He died around the year 650.

In approximately the same time period, another Irish saint, Adamnán, who came from County Donegal, 'departed from out his body on the feast of John Baptist.' He describes heaven as being full of light and covered in a beautiful fragrance – a joyous, noble and splendid place where only happiness reigns. The Lord exudes splendour, brightness and loveliness. His appearance is described as 'a fiery mass,' 'seven times as radiant as the sun' and 'burning on forever.' He has 'a radiance as of a royal star' encircling him.

Adamnán is also taken to hell, with its many horrors. The sounds of wailing and moaning are everywhere. Instantly – 'in the twinkling of an eye' – Adamnán is then led 'whereunto he had been brought at first, after his departure from the body.' From there he returns to earth, to his bodily form, and continues to preach about what he had seen during his many visits to Ireland, and also in Iona. His death is believed to have occurred in 704.

A third, and final, near-death experience with widespread appeal throughout Ireland – this time in the Middle Ages – involves a nobleman and knight from Cashel by the name of Tundale. By all accounts, he was a sad and miserable soul. Although from a distinguished family and possessing a cheerful appearance and elegant manner, he was described as cruel, neglectful of the Church, mean to the poor and a friend to 'buffoons, mimes and jesters.'

The story is told how, one day, Tundale travelled to Cork to retrieve a debt. While there, he collapsed. Attempts to resuscitate him failed. Arrangements were made for his burial. Fortunately, those who worked on reviving him noticed what they thought was a small patch of heat on one side of his body. His burial was delayed as a result. It proved to be a wise decision as, following a period of three days, Tundale recovered to explain how his soul had separated from his body and he had embarked on a voyage to the other side.

Tundale describes heaven as being wonderfully scented, full of flowers and open fields, bright and pleasant. The sun shines and the inhabitants are beautiful, 'without spot or wrinkle' and dressed in white, precious robes. Everybody is happy and joyful. There is no sadness. Choruses of saints, dressed in brilliant white, sing their praises to God. 'The white of their garments was as white as snow struck by the radiance of the sun,' we are told. He is filled with joy.

Although anxious to stay, Tundale is ordered to return to earth and to re-enter his body. Immediately he felt the weight of his body and perceived himself to be back in its form. His eyes opened, he sighed and he came back a changed and God-fearing man. 'Is this not the spirit going and returning?' everyone gasped, bringing to a close the most comprehensive near-death experience ever recorded in Ireland.

The interest of Irish people in near-death and out-of-body experiences waned in the Victorian era. At the time, both the middle classes and the ascendancy were obsessed with spirits and ghosts and the issue of how to communicate with the dead. Ireland was captivated by the supernatural. Séances, involving spiritualists attempting to make contact with the deceased, became fashionable. Clairvoyants were in wide-spread demand.

This intense fascination with what was often referred to as 'spiritism' was hardly surprising. Victorians, having already invented the wireless, telephone, typewriter, gramophone, bicycle, petrol-driven car and steam train, among thousands of other useful things, understandably felt confident of conquering the new frontier beyond the grave. Everything, it was believed, was possible.

The American, Thomas Edison, who invented the light bulb, tried his hand at constructing a machine to contact the spirit world. Dublin was abuzz with the progress being made. The poet W. B. Yeats enthused over a new apparatus – which he referred to as the 'metallic homunculus' – purportedly designed to receive and amplify voices from the other side. So confident was Yeats in the product that he referred to it as potentially 'the greatest discovery of the modern world.'

There was another reason why spiritualism rather than near-death or out-of-body experiences dominated the Victorian era. The reality at the time was that the state of medical science was far from conducive to surviving near-death. Few heart attack patients outlived their ordeal. Most died. Medical advances involving resuscitation, ECGs, drugs, and especially the use of defibrillators to shock the heart back into a normal rhythm had yet to be perfected. Cardiac arrest patients had, as a result, considerably less chance to recover and to tell their tales.

In the circumstances, near-death visions – which are also examined later in this book – became an object of great fascination. It was widely reported and believed at the time that deceased family and friends came to welcome the dying to the other side. Societies such as the Dublin Hermetic Society and the Dublin Theosophical Society spent many evenings discussing the topic.

Extensive research was undertaken by Sir William Barrett, who was Professor of Physics at the Royal College of Science in Dublin. During the period when Barrett conducted his inquiries, in the late 1800s and early 1900s, the Royal College of Science had yet to be absorbed into University College Dublin, where it eventually formed the basis of the Science Faculty.

Barrett, in *Death-Bed Visions*, which was published in 1926 but contained material mostly collected decades earlier, relates some remarkable stories of visions witnessed by the dying shortly before death. He especially chronicles meetings with relatives and friends – an element that would later be identified as part of the classic near-death experience. Among his case histories is a story from 1906 detailing the death of a young boy, aged nine.

The boy, we are told, had recently undergone an operation from which he failed to recover. Despite his condition he was perfectly rational and lucid, fully aware of the presence of his mother, the nurse and the doctor. Knowing he was dying, he held his mother's hands. After a short time he looked up and asked her if she too could see his little sister in the room. 'No, where is she?' his mother asked, aware that his sister had died four years before his birth. 'Right over there. She is looking at me,' he responded.

The boy then exclaimed that he could see a deceased adult acquaintance along with a young friend who had died about a year beforehand. 'I'm going to them,' he said. 'I don't want to leave you, but you'll come to me soon, won't you? Open the door and let them in. They are waiting outside.' Immediately after saying this, he died.

Barrett also identified a further element that would later be recognised as a component of the near-death experience – the barrier, border or boundary. One story he relates concerns a woman who, close to death, spoke of seeing her deceased mother and father, her brother and sisters, among others. 'Can't you see them?' she asked her husband, who could not. She then added, 'Part of our family have crossed the flood, and soon the other part will be gathered home, and then we shall be a family complete in heaven!'

Further stories – this time relating to visitations occurring shortly after death – surfaced from other unlikely yet credible sources. Dan Breen, describing his life as a guerrilla fighter during the struggle for national independence, wrote how his comrade Seán Treacy, who had just been shot dead, appeared to him at the foot of his hospital bed. At the time, Breen was confined to the Mater Hospital in Dublin and had no knowledge that Treacy had been killed in an ambush in nearby Talbot Street.

'I am not given either to superstition or to flights of imagination,' Breen wrote in his 1924 autobiography *My Fight For Irish Freedom*, 'and yet I knew beyond any shadow of doubt that Seán Treacy was dead. I saw him standing at the foot of my bed with a radiant smile on his countenance. Towards nightfall Mick Collins came to see me. "Where is Seán?" I asked. Mick averted his eyes and replied, "He's out in the country." Ten days passed before I learned the full story.'

Similar accounts were commonplace throughout the first half of the twentieth century. Dan Keane, from County Kerry, recalled for me an event which took place around the death of his father in 1941. Dan was aged 21 at the time. 'My father had TB of the throat,' Dan remembers. 'A few nights before he died I heard him say that he saw his father, who had died in 1918, at the foot of the bed. That was only a few days before he passed away.

'My father was very sick with TB but he had his senses about him. He said it to more than one of us. We didn't question him and he made no remark only that he was there. We had heard of things like that before, of people seeing other people, especially their parents, when they were dying. They would see their parents coming to them. It was common.'

It wasn't until much later in the twentieth century – the 1970s – that perceptions concerning death were turned upside down by startling revelations from America. At the centre of the storm was a groundbreaking book by businessman Robert Monroe in which he described how he had frequently floated outside of his body. His adventures, he explained, had begun one day back in 1958 when he became detached from his physical form. Panic-stricken and fearful that he was dead, he forced himself into a speedy return. Similar events happened regularly after that.

Monroe's disclosures were, in truth, far from new. What he described had in earlier times been referred to as 'astral travel'. Similar spectacular happenings were known and noted as far back as ancient Egypt, where etchings and drawings portrayed images of the 'Ka', or astral body, leaving the physical form. Other references can be found in ancient writings from India, China and Tibet. Indeed, it can be said that the Irish legend of Mog Ruith – the blind Druid from Munster who could fly through the sky to work his spells against his enemies – was rooted in the concept of astral travel.

Monroe, in his book *Journeys Out Of The Body*, introduced the phenomenon to a new audience. The influence of his book, which was published in 1971, was startling. It brought to public attention common occurrences that had become buried and suppressed over the centuries. Monroe called them 'out-of-body experiences'. Later, in 1974, he set up the Monroe Institute in Virginia, USA, which to the present day examines issues surrounding human consciousness.

The floodgates opened, with people who were previously fearful of being seen as mad or delusionary stepping forward to tell their tales. They described how they had departed from their bodies sometimes during illness or following a major trauma. Often there was no obvious reason at all. Many reported leaving their bodies while asleep. Most could recall vivid details of what had happened below. Some explained how they had passed with ease through walls and other obstacles.

Many of the stories were highly convincing. One of the best known involved a heart attack patient in the USA, named

Maria, who featured in Kimberly Clark Sharp's book *After The Light*. The woman – a middle-aged Hispanic migrant worker – explained how, following a coronary, she had watched herself being resuscitated while floating up near the ceiling. She provided, in vivid detail, a description of the resuscitation procedures and the conversations between medical staff, along with information concerning the equipment that was used.

She also explained how she had travelled outside the hospital, where she saw a man's dark blue tennis shoe, which was well-worn, scuffed near the left little toe and with a lace caught under the heel, sitting on a window-ledge some three stories above the ground. Her social worker – the book's author Kimberly Clark Sharp – was intrigued. She checked three sides of the hospital before locating the shoe.

'I was four rooms into the west side of the building when I pressed my face against a window-pane, peered down on yet another ledge, and felt my heart go *thunk*. There it was,' Kimberly Clark Sharp reported. She also concluded that the only way Maria could have described the shoe, and its details, was by hovering in mid-air, three stories up, and directly in front of the shoe!

The world had barely come to terms with the concept of out-of-body travel when a new study arrived on the scene. The book *Life After Life*, which was published in 1975, explored near-death experiences and had instant public appeal. Compiled by a young American named Dr. Raymond Moody, it was based on more than 100 case studies of people who had reached the point of death and survived.

Moody, for the very first time, coined the phrase 'near-death experience'. Like Monroe, he gave definition to a phenomenon that had been occurring for thousands of years but in modern times had been suppressed and concealed.

People – to put it plainly – had, before Moody, feared being regarded as mentally unsound if they divulged their personal accounts. The book's publication also 'created a worldwide change in our understanding of death,' as one eminent medical expert put it.

The origins of *Life After Life* were simple. While studying philosophy in Virginia, Moody attended a talk by psychiatrist Dr. George Ritchie, who related a remarkable story. Ritchie, it transpired, had been declared dead after contracting double pneumonia but had been successfully revived. He described how he had left his body, entered a brilliant light that emanated love, and reviewed all the events of his life in a grand panorama.

Later, when lecturing at the University of Virginia, one of Moody's students told him of another experience featuring details that were almost identical. More and more evidence eventually came his way. Remarkably, the accounts all shared characteristics in common – the sense of being dead, the bodily separation, the feeling of peace, right through to the tunnel, the bright light, meeting deceased relatives and friends, encountering a 'superior being', and a reluctance to return to the world of the living.

The reaction to the book, from scientists and sceptics, was savage and swift. Many questioned the nature of near-death experiences, arguing that they were in reality a form of mental illness. More suggested the phenomenon happened only to religious fanatics. Others claimed that they were, at best, hallucinatory or rare. Denial was commonplace.

A doctor who attended one of Moody's lectures asked the first question from the floor at the lecture's conclusion. 'I have been in medicine for a long time,' he began. 'If these experiences are as common as you say they are, why haven't I heard of them?' Hoping that someone else in the audience might have encountered one, Moody asked, 'Has anyone else here heard of anything like this?' To which the doctor's wife raised her hand and told how a very close friend of theirs had once had a near-death experience!

To this day, a heated debate has ensued, with opposing camps holding widely-conflicting views. The controversy is a complex one, rooted on the one hand in biological, chemical and psychological research, and on the other hand in spiritual truths professed down through the centuries. Both sets of arguments will be examined towards the end of this book.

The debate, as we will see, is expansive, stretching all the way back to Fursa, Adamnán and Tundale, and further still to the Old and New Testaments, the Koran and other sacred texts with their expositions about the hereafter. The ancient Sanskrit Hindu scripture Bhagavad Gita puts the spiritual case well: 'Never was there a time when you did not exist and there will never be a time when you cease to exist.'

The dispute, at the end of the day, is inconclusive. As Moody says, near-death experiences might well be 'a glimpse into another plane of reality. But is that life after life? I just don't know.' Ultimately, in the absence of definitive proof, the decision can only be yours. The evidence lies in the pages ahead.

THE NEAR-DEATH EXPERIENCE

A wonderful story is told about a fish and a turtle who wanted to know what it's like to live on dry land. The fish persuaded the turtle to give it a try. He crawled out of the shallows and returned a short time later. 'So what is it like to live on dry land?' asked the fish. 'Well,' said the turtle, 'the hot, dry sand is completely different from the wet sand on our seabed. And the flowers and plants are totally different from our seaweed.

'What's more,' the turtle explained, 'walking through air is entirely different from swimming through water.' 'So what is it like to live on dry land?' the fish asked once again. 'Unfortunately,' the perplexed turtle replied, 'there is nothing in our experience to relate it to.'

This ancient parable, which will be familiar to Buddhists, is worth bearing in mind when evaluating the stories of those who have gone through a near-death experience. What they have seen, sensed and encountered is often beyond anything describable or comprehensible on earth. Time, for them, has slowed to a crawl. In a matter of seconds, or less than a minute, while 'dead', they have gleaned a kaleidoscope of insights and revelations light years beyond the norm.

In addition to the sensations linked to their travels, they have felt a vast range of intense emotions while making knife-edge decisions concerning living and dying. Some have undertaken life reviews spanning decades and involving myriad events – in fragments of real time. All have glimpsed beyond the curtain to where we end up when we die.

On their return, their lives, in the main, are profoundly and lastingly changed. Their existence takes on a new purpose. Most develop a deep concern for others and for discovering the meaning of life. The vast majority become intensely spiritual although many veer away from established religions. Virtually all lose their fear of death and face the prospect of dying without dread or apprehension.

Studies show that two out of three believe their lives have been significantly transformed. Some, sadly, find it impossible to cope with the life they return to. Above all, most struggle to articulate the sensations and emotions they felt during their journeys, leading to considerable frustration. Fortunately the following have made the effort, and these are their stories.

MARK KELLY **lost both legs in a bomb blast in Glengormley, County Antrim, at the height of the Troubles back in August 1976. Aged 18 years, he experienced a most vivid journey to the afterlife.**

I was a youth worker at the time and we had the opportunity to keep the youth club open over the summer months. It hadn't been done in previous years but it was something I had lobbied for. I didn't go to the Fleadh Cheoil in Buncrana that weekend, as I was supposed to do. Instead we were trying to prove just how trustworthy we could be operating our youth club. So we were engaged in a lot of work including painting and wiring things up like disco lights.

A fellow had taken a set of keys and forgotten to give them back to me. I went over to the pub to get them, so that we could lock up. I was in a part of the pub that I wouldn't normally be in, one of the back lounges. Someone bought me a pint. Somewhere in the course of that, three boys came in and left a bomb sewn in the sleeve of a jacket, more or less beside me. It went off.

I was lying in the pub and then I came around. There was an acrid smell in the aftermath of the bomb. I couldn't move. I shouted, 'Help!' I kept shouting it. I was shouting, 'Help! I want my mum!' Security forces were concerned about secondary devices but, when they heard the voice, a reserve RUC man decided to take the bull by the horns and come in and get me out. They carried me out on a door.

It was an August night, not too hot at all, and when I felt the summer chill in the air that's when the pain hit. My God! It was bad! I knew I was injured and I couldn't see. I had been blinded either by the flash or the debris in my eyes. My hearing was partially affected. I wasn't even aware of what had happened. I kept asking to get up and go to the toilet but they kept asking me my name and address and details, ad nauseam. I told them many times but they were probably trying to keep me conscious.

I could really feel the pain and I can remember every ramp to the hospital. There were these security ramps that had been put in place to slow traffic down at flashpoints. When I got to the hospital and got that smell of ether, I passed out. I already had a sense I had lost my legs. I don't know whether I had heard someone say it or what. But I was happy to be alive because, while I was probably the worst injury in that bomb blast, so many people hadn't survived other bombs.

Eventually I was coming around well. Members of the youth club were coming up to visit. But I just wanted to get out into the fresh air and wasn't at all happy with being in the hospital. I wanted to escape. Then I took a downturn. I developed osteomyelitis. There was a three-litre abscess in my stump. You can imagine a three-litre bottle of Coke! I could have died at that point.

Somewhere around that time, I gave up and decided to go. There was no more fight in me. So one evening, in the quiet of the ward, I decided I was going to make my peace and I started on this journey. I saw a bright, welcoming light. It was very bright, white and pure. I couldn't say it was star-shaped and it certainly wasn't just a circle. It had a radiance coming from the circumference.

I was in motion and going towards it. It was as if I was in a narrowing tunnel although I couldn't see walls. It was dark. Everything was dark except for the light. The tunnel was converging on the light. The light was the focus. I was drifting and all the time I was going towards it and it wasn't coming to me. It wasn't a body I was travelling in. I had a sense of coming out of my body. It might have been my soul or whatever. I haven't a clue.

I felt I was on a journey and going towards a better place. The journey was slow. It was incredibly peaceful. I had no fear. I had no anxiety. I just had a desire to go there. I wanted to follow the course. There was an acceptance within myself that I was leaving and following the journey.

I got a sense of a broad expanse of water. It was like a broad, dark river. I felt I was going across it. Somewhere in the journey across it, I saw people in front of me. I couldn't say that I recognised anybody but it was as if I knew the people. I didn't see them as angels. They were almost human in form. They were welcoming. Although I don't remember anything they said, I do remember activity with open arms and the feeling that they were saying, 'Everything is OK.'

Then from behind – probably from the bank of the river I had come across or from the start of the expanse of water – there were voices. These were the voices of the young people in Glengormley. Once I heard the voices I became anxious. A doubt started to come into my mind. I thought that if I were to continue the journey it was all over.

The voices got louder. They were persuasive. I thought, 'It's make your mind up time.' It took a huge amount of energy to pull myself out and come to a decision that now wasn't the time to go. It didn't feel like I was being analytical. It was like my thinking process was at a different level. It was as if there was something more for me to do or be involved in. I felt it wasn't my time.

I pulled myself out of it and I was exhausted. I was probably already at the point of exhaustion going into the journey, deciding it was time to go or accepting it was time to go. It had also taken some effort to decide, 'Now is not the time to continue the journey.' So I was truly exhausted when I came back. I felt a mixture of emotions. Relief was there and probably the realisation that it wasn't the time to depart although I couldn't have explained why.

It was an incredible experience. It's something I haven't thought about in maybe ten years but it's not something I should probably let go. Sometimes it doesn't do any harm to bring myself back to it. I know some people say these things are drug induced and there are different consultants with different notions. But it wasn't drug induced. I know that. I know it was a conscious decision that it was time to leave. It was also a conscious decision to not continue the journey.

I certainly have a sense, since then, that there's a life after death. But in the hospital I didn't get the feeling that I was a Catholic going towards my maker. There was no religion about the whole thing. Instead it gave me a sense of a 'greater being'. I do believe in a higher power, an absolute being, God, or whatever terminology you want to put on it, but I think it's about the one God, everybody's God. And I don't have a fear of death. I'm on borrowed time. But that time, back in 1976, it just wasn't time to depart.

MICHELLE, FROM COUNTY GALWAY, describes her near-death experience during a difficult childbirth.

Back in 2000 I was pregnant, at the age of 30. I was living in the States at the time and coming up to having my very first child. I went in to have the baby. The next thing there was an emergency going on. The baby wasn't coming out naturally and they had to rush me in to do a Caesarean. I was then brought into the recovery room.

I suddenly started to get fierce pain. It was just like the contractions all over again. My mother had come over from Ireland for the birth of her first grandchild. I said to her, 'I could swear I'm having another baby.' I had terrible cramps. She went out and called a nurse. The nurse came in and said, 'No, she's fine, she's fine.'

The pains kept getting worse and worse and worse. My mother started to panic and started screaming at the nurses' station, 'Please come in and look at her!' At this stage I had started to go pale and my lips and nails had started to go blue.

They lifted up the covers and they could see I was haemorrhaging very badly. They rushed me into the operating room and they tried to stop the bleeding. They thought it had worked but I started haemorrhaging again. They rushed me back down to the operating theatre again and this time there was mayhem in the area.

I was going in and out of consciousness. At one stage the midwife was grabbing my face and saying, 'Stay with me, Michelle! Stay with me! Look at my face! Please stay with me!' I remember her face so vividly. I knew there was mayhem around me but I was trying to focus on this face.

I suddenly went from the mayhem to utter peace and quiet and calmness. I felt I was floating. I went to another place. It was an open space, with a creamy light. It wasn't a very bright, blinding light. Instead it was soothing and peaceful. I wasn't scared.

Blowing in front of me was what I can only describe as a linen panel or a curtain. It was blowing as if the wind was coming from behind it or from the side of it. It was like a hot summer's day with a soft breeze blowing. Everything was in slow motion. I was moving left to right and just floating past the curtain. I was so close to the curtain that I could see the criss-cross of the weave in front of me.

As I got to the end of the panel or curtain, I floated past it to the side but didn't cross the line. Just beyond the line were my mother-in-law and father-in-law, who had both passed away. They had died only a few years before and I was close to both of them. They were on the other side, standing off in the distance. There was nothing else there, just the two of them.

They were standing not too far away but far enough that I couldn't touch them. They didn't say anything. They just stood there smiling and looking at me. When I saw them I went to go over. But my mother-in-law, Barbara, put both her hands up as if to say, 'Stop!' She shook her head very kindly, as if to say, 'Not now! Go back!' I thought of my baby and knew I had to return.

I then woke up in Intensive Care on a life-support machine. I couldn't really open my eyes. My face was bloated. I remember the doctor saying, 'I'm sorry, we can't even give her 50-50 tonight.' People were crying. But all I was trying to do was tell people where I had been.

I was trying to make signs with my hands. I was writing on their arms. First of all I wrote, 'I-C-E' because I was so dry.

But they said, 'No, Michelle, we can't give you anything.' Then I wrote, 'I-C-U' and they said, 'Yes, you are in ICU.' Then, with my finger on their arm, I wrote 'B-A-R-B-A-R-A' and just pointed to myself. I was pointing into my eyes to explain to them what I had seen.

About two or three days later they took me off the life-support and I was choking and spluttering and saying, 'I have to tell you where I was and what I saw!' My father had been called over from Ireland, at this stage, because they thought I wasn't going to make it. Everyone was sitting around. The doctors were there as well.

One of the doctors said, 'In all the years I've been a doctor – and I've been a doctor here for 37 years – I have never come across what happened to you. You ended up bleeding to death, basically. You flatlined for ten seconds. Only for the fact that the anaesthesiologist was quick-thinking, and took a straw and started breathing in through your mouth for you, you would have been gone.'

It was when they told me that I had flatlined for ten seconds that my eyes widened and I said, 'So what I experienced was real.' I knew I had gone some place and something had happened.

Eventually I moved back to Ireland with my son. Life has been good ever since. I feel the magic around me every day. I know just how lucky I was to come back and to have a second chance. I really want to enjoy every day now. It's not about material things – it's about things that matter, like having dinner together or sitting out and having a cup of tea.

I have pushed out negativity from my life. Anybody who doesn't have nice words to say about other people, I don't have them in my life anymore. I think life is too short for that. I think those are the secrets in life that will make you a happier person.

I was brought up in a Catholic house and went to mass but I wouldn't have been an avid mass-goer and I still am not. I wouldn't feel that I need to go to church more often. It's amazing how the God that everyone else is telling us we should be praying to is not the one that I see. Instead I am very much more spiritual but not in a religious way.

I have also lost my fear of death. I once had to go and see an uncle of mine when he was dying. When I walked into the room, he passed away. Even though I was crying, I felt the comfort of knowing where he went. I used to have a terrible fear of death but I now don't think about it, don't worry about it and don't fear it anymore. There's no fear left in me because I know where I'm going next time.

DOMINIC, FROM THE WEST OF IRELAND, travelled through a large tunnel following a haemorrhage experienced while undergoing major surgery.

I had a heart condition as a student but then I was OK and I got about 36 years out of it. Unfortunately I relapsed. I found out that not only did I need a valve but I had an aneurysm of my aortic root. The aneurysm was ready to pop. Eventually they managed to get me a bed and get me in. I was seen in August and the surgeon was going on holidays in September, so the operation was planned for after that.

Very soon, my secretary began to notice that I wasn't that great and I was getting much more tired. I think she contacted the hospital and I got a phone call on a Monday saying there was a vacancy for the Wednesday and if I was in on the Tuesday they would do it. I remember saying to the chap who rang me, 'Could you give me 24 hours to think?' He said, 'I can't even give you 24 minutes. You must say yes or no now.' So I said, 'Yes.'

They operated and I was under anaesthetic. There was a whole team working on me. They had my chest split wide open on the table. Then the surgeon just touched the aneurysm and it popped. It blew all over the place. He was covered in blood. He couldn't even see out through his goggles at times. It must have been like a slaughterhouse. The surgeon told me later that it was so bad that once he got the bleeding under control he had to go out and re-gown, take every stitch off, and come back in and start again.

At that time I experienced a huge sound in my head. It was like a clanging, metallic sound. If you remember the film *Dirty Harry*, Clint Eastwood was chasing a guy one night and the guy was in some kind of a stadium. It was absolutely pitch black in there. Suddenly Clint Eastwood's detective partner spotted where the lights came on. So he pulled this shaft and there was a huge 'clank'. You could hear it in the film. That's the sort of 'clank' I heard.

It became so bright, so quickly, as if somebody had just switched something on. I wasn't looking down on the theatre, on myself being operated on, or anything like that. Instead I was in this place. I was walking down a street. It was tunnel shaped but it was quite wide. It was as wide as any street in Ireland but it was dome shaped, as if you were in a huge tunnel. The way we normally think of tunnels is of very small places but this was huge with what was almost a roof across it. Everything was totally still and totally empty. The only person there was me.

I didn't see any houses or anything like that. I didn't look to my left or my right. I was just looking straight on. Everything was black but at the very end of the street you could see this huge bright light. It was intensely bright and circular. It was like a complete full moon, blocking the entrance to this tunnel shaped road. The tunnel was, say, 20 metres across and maybe 50 metres high and then you had the end of that tunnel being blocked by this total brightness.

I was walking towards the light, down the street, with my hands in my pockets, fully clothed, and I said to myself, 'I wonder where I'm going now?' I remember the way I was walking with my legs rotated outwards. When we were kids we used to go to Charlie Chaplin films and they used to be the funniest films I ever saw. I was walking the same way as Charlie Chaplin, with his gammy walk. The other thing about it was that I was totally alone. There was nobody else on the street and I had no fear whatsoever. I felt happy and content. I was just very curious.

I never made it to the end of the street but I kept on thinking, 'I wonder where I'm going?' It kept reverberating in my mind. My mind was very active and curious. That went on for a while. Then I disappeared out of the tunnel. The next thing I knew I was back, being wheeled out of the theatre. My wife and one of my sons were there telling me I was OK. My son was telling me, 'Dad, it's all over, you're back.'

I was so sick at the time, I couldn't think much about it during the first ten days. Then I began to wonder what I had seen. It was probably ten or twelve days post-op before it came through my head. I didn't say much about it to anybody. I just kept it to myself. I didn't know about this sort of thing beforehand. There was nothing to precondition me or anything like that.

The surgeon eventually said to me, 'You were dead for 40 seconds. You had no recordable blood pressure.' At that stage I put two and two together and I said, 'That must be when I was walking down the street. I must have been dead. That's what happened.' I suppose I just had a voyage and I came back. So I think I was very, very lucky. If the surgeon hadn't got the situation under control, I'd say I would have seen the end of the tunnel. There is no doubt.

I don't really know what to think about it. I'm not even too keen to get interested in it. But I realise my chest was wide open and I can't imagine how I was conscious at the same time – particularly when I was dead! I also wonder if I had got any further down that road where would I have been? As for the image of Charlie Chaplin, I have wondered when you are dying are you transported back to the happiest days of your life? Thank God I never got the chance to find out fully.

I think it has changed me somewhat. I would be much more considerate towards people. It's almost as if I know I'm not alone and I have a duty to be more considerate. I'd also be a bit more confident about a God as a result. Not that I'm a mad religious person but I'd have more belief. All I really know is that this is what it is like to die. The only person there is you.

I used to have a saying years ago, 'When you are dying, you die by yourself.' There might be people around your bed but you are the one that's doing the dying. That's the way it was. There's no one there in the tunnel except you. But it certainly wasn't bad. And death is nothing to be frightened about. Only time will tell, I suppose, but it should be good news.

JOHN, FROM COUNTY ROSCOMMON, had his experience back in 1994. He was aged 18 at the time.

I was in a takeaway with some friends. There were four of us altogether. It was during the day. We were sitting down, just getting some food and stuff and laughing. I remember there were three other guys sitting at another table – they were workmen. It's all so clear in my mind, so vivid.

Suddenly I got a piece of burger caught in my throat. All my friends were still laughing but I was overwhelmed by fear and horror. I couldn't talk or communicate so I started slapping my back in the hope that they might see I had a problem and know what to do. They thought I was joking and they kept on laughing. My friend later told me that my colour changed. I was going blue from the lack of blood to my brain.

Panic was setting in. My vision was deteriorating. So was my hearing. I clambered over seats and fell onto my knees. Somebody shouted, 'Get an ambulance!' The woman behind the counter started ringing for one. Other people started shouting. The more they shouted the more panicky they sounded. When I heard them being panicky I got more panicky. I said to myself, 'This is unbelievable. I'm going to die here.'

Everything suddenly went black. I was conscious of being in a black void. It was the darkest black I had ever seen in my life. It was like liquid black, the pure absence of everything – of sound, emotion and feeling. I had no fear at all. All my fear had disappeared.

I was no longer aware that I had a body. I couldn't feel my legs or arms or anything. I remember saying to myself, 'This is what it must be like to be dead.' It seemed like I was that way for a half an hour but I couldn't have been because I learned later that I was unconscious for nine-and-a-half minutes.

In the distance I could see this sort of white thing. I said, 'What's that?' As I concentrated on it, it looked like a little diamond. It was really bright but you could still look at it. It was pure white, unlike anything I had ever seen. It was miles away but it stood out because I was in this black.

I was concentrating on it and thinking, 'That's really beautiful.' I was saying, 'Maybe I should try and go towards it.' So I willed myself nearer to it. I wasn't aware of having any legs so the only way I could get to it was by willing myself mentally to approach it. As I got to it I felt a sort of joyous feeling. I thought, 'This feels familiar.'

I suddenly saw little photographs of things in my life. There were photos of my mum and my sisters and different things like that. It was like looking at little snapshots with no movement in them. It might be a face or an experience or a memory. There was one with my sister holding the white cat she had as a kid. There was another of me on a boat with my uncle and my dad. They were crystal clear photographs, one after the other.

I felt I was being prompted to remember my family. I could feel the emotion that was felt at the time when the various things happened. Like, when I saw the photo of my sister with the cat, I could feel the emotion that she was feeling even though I wasn't present at the time. It was very strange.

At this stage I had slowed down on my approach to the light. I could look into it. It was like looking into a sun although it wouldn't hurt your eyes. Then I heard a voice. I couldn't make out if it was a man or a woman. It said, 'You are going to be OK!' Whoever said it put their hands out to stop me from progressing further. It was like a restriction but I couldn't see anybody. The voice sounded familiar even though I hadn't heard it before.

I withdrew back from the diamond of light. I then remember waking up on the floor of the takeaway with everybody standing around me. I was literally shaking like a leaf. The piece of burger had come up on its own out of my throat. It had come out onto the floor. That must have happened when the voice said I was going to be OK. The ambulance people then came and they said I was fine.

Afterwards I had a real feeling that everything was crystal

clear and that life was precious. I developed a new-found appreciation for life. I have mellowed a lot. I still have my moments but I have changed. I'm not really a religious person but, after what occurred, I believe there is something. What happened has convinced me 110 per cent that this life isn't all there is to it. There is a purpose to everything.

I'd love to know what would have happened if I got to the diamond. People say that if you go there you can't come back. I definitely think something happened that day and I was on the way out if not dead already. It's constantly on my mind. It's as vivid as if it happened yesterday although it happened a long time ago, in April 1994.

MONICA, FROM COUNTY LIMERICK, also had a life review as part of her experience.

I had a miscarriage just after Christmas 1978. I already had a little boy aged one year and eleven months and a little girl aged twelve months at the time. I started to bleed very heavily and could not summon help as our house was in a very isolated area and a telephone wasn't available. My husband had gone to get the car repaired at a friend's garage, so I could not contact him either.

I changed and fed the little ones and put them in their cots for safety, as I felt so weak. I prayed and begged the Sacred Heart to help me. Thankfully, and quite unexpectedly, my sister and her husband arrived from England and decided on the spur of the moment to visit me. That was a miracle in itself as I am from a large family and they could easily have decided to visit another member of the family first.

As I arrived at the hospital I felt so light-headed and terribly weak. I was bleeding non-stop. I was attended to immediately. Apparently the medical team said I was very lucky as I would have bled to death in a very short while. I didn't have any pain at any stage but I felt myself just fading away. I received an injection in my arm and immediately felt an awful sensation as its contents pounded through my veins.

They were proceeding to wheel me up the corridor when suddenly I experienced this beautiful calmness and smelled the most fabulous scent of flowers. It wasn't like perfume but more like the scent you get in a fresh garden of flowers after a shower of rain. I then felt my mind, or soul, or spirit rise above my body and I found myself looking down from the ceiling at my body and the medical team.

I was up by the big lights that you find in a hospital. I was looking down at the crown of my head first and then down my body to my toes. I was fully aware of what was happening around me. There was no noise, just a beautiful quietness. All the banging and clattering of the hospital had stopped. I felt so happy and excited.

Then I saw flashes of events from my life. It was like some sort of a review starting with my teenage years. They were very happy times in my life. The best way I can describe it is that it was like flicking through a photo album and experiencing again all the thoughts and emotions I had experienced when the photos were taken. The photos were in black and white and were kind of over on my right-hand side.

I saw one scene where I was out dancing, which I loved. I was jiving. I could feel the excitement inside me again. I saw myself when I was young going to school with my sister. There was nothing negative and there was nothing in my life I was ashamed of or guilty about. My life was being relived and I have to say I felt incredibly happy. I didn't want to come back.

I was fully aware that the medical team were trying to wake me up as I was looking down at them. I remember feeling compassion for them as they were so kind to me. I can so clearly remember wondering why they didn't realise I was dead and that they were wasting their time. Only one thing bothered me and that was the fact that I wasn't smiling. I wanted people to see how happy I was and I regretted not having a smile on my face.

Suddenly I thought of my little babies that I had left at home that morning. I knew they needed me so much to look after them. I so wanted to continue on whatever journey I was on but the need of my children was very much on my mind. As soon as I realised this fact, I found myself sliding back into my body. I actually think that if I didn't have my two children at home, I wouldn't now be alive.

It was as if I made the decision myself that I had to go back. I found myself waking up. All the noises and voices of the hospital resumed and I heard the doctor calling my name. I do not know how long my experience went on for but I guess it was pretty quick as we were still in the corridor when I returned.

The experience has changed my life. It lives on with me and hopefully has made me a more compassionate, caring person. I turn the other cheek and people will even remark to me that I would be nice to people that maybe wouldn't be nice to me. But I do it because I know that someday everything I do and say in this life will be reviewed by me again when I leave this world for good and my aim is to get to heaven.

When I am near a person that is dying now, I almost envy the beautiful experience that is awaiting them. I recently knew a priest who died and I just gave him a hug and said, 'Be happy. Where you are going, you wouldn't want to come back.' I never cry for a person that is dead. It's a new beginning and they wouldn't want to return.

EDDIE, FROM COUNTY MEATH, almost died when he was shot during an armed robbery at his home. He had a near-death experience while in critical condition in hospital.

I was shot twice. The two bullets went in the front, just below the heart, and went out the back, beside my spine. They took a lot of my insides with them. Bullets make a very small hole when they go in but when they go out the back they bring lots of stuff with them.

I had a damaged left lung. I lost my spleen. Half my liver was gone. There was loads of liver coming up my throat when I was going in the ambulance and it was going into a basin. They weren't too concerned about the liver because they said it would grow again. I lost a lot of my stomach as well.

I was fighting for my life for the next two months. At the time I was hoping to die. It seemed so easy. I knew I only had to close my eyes and not come back. I remember, one day, a nurse came by and I grabbed her dress and said, 'I'm going to get sick.' I got a haemorrhage and blood just poured out of my throat. It was a huge haemorrhage. Everyone panicked.

They started running around, doing things. They ran out of blood for me. I heard the doctor saying, 'I need blood!' They rang up looking for blood and they were told, 'We can't give you blood because we're closed at night.' He said, 'I'll send a motorcyclist up.' They said, 'No, we can't do that.' He said, 'But I've got a man dying!' I was lying there, saying, 'That's me!'

My wife was pushing to get me transferred to Dublin. The local hospital didn't want to let me go. The next day I found myself in an ambulance, with a nurse sitting next to me, and the siren was on. I looked out behind and I could see one of my friends behind the ambulance trying to keep up with it.

I remember going into the hospital in Dublin, lying back

on a stretcher. They put me in this big ward. I was the centre of attention. A nurse sat opposite me, just looking, to keep an eye on me. That night I haemorrhaged again. I remember waving and a nurse brought a basin over quickly. They didn't give me much hope of recovery, only about two per cent. But they said, 'We'll do the best we can.' I then had two operations.

I don't know whether it was during the first or second operation that I had a strange experience. I was in this tunnel. I was going on a sort of a conveyor belt, like the belt at an airport. You know where the cases go through at the airport, there's a cover there where your suitcases go. It's like a flap or a cover. You can't see the other side of it because there is darkness there. It was exactly like that.

I was lying on the belt with my arms outstretched and I was heading for this flap. There was no light, just darkness beyond the opening I was heading towards. I couldn't see beyond but it was like some kind of a void. To me it was just a dark place but maybe it was meant to be hell or someplace. I don't know. It certainly didn't feel like heaven. I was moving along what I call this tunnel and I was quite contented. But when I came to the entrance to go in, my arms stopped me and I came to a halt.

There were loads of mass cards and greeting cards floating around above me. They were drifting around in the air. I was just lying back, reading them as they floated above my eyes. In the local hospital there were lots of mass cards and get well cards that people had sent in. The hospital didn't know where to put them. They were all over the place. They were from my friends. It was like these were the same cards.

I was just looking at the cards and saying, 'Yeah, that's from so-and-so and so-and-so.' They were there long enough to read. All this time my arms were still out sideways so I

41

couldn't get into the opening to the tunnel. My arms stopped me going through the trapdoor. The next thing I was back in my bed and woke up again with this strange feeling.

I didn't think much about it at the time. It's only afterwards that I looked back on it and asked, 'Was this real or not?' I told a few people and I told my wife but most people looked at me funny. I don't know what it was. I think I was probably dying at the time. I was on my way out. I was going but something stopped me.

It made me know there's a God up there and that somebody is very fond of me or loves me. I know the doctors did the best they could but I wouldn't have survived without some other help from elsewhere. My faith has probably been stronger afterwards. I look back and say, 'Thanks, God! I know you are there!'

Also, before the shooting I would have been a bit concerned about dying but afterwards it didn't bother me in the least. I could die so contented, just close my eyes and drift off, although it would be difficult leaving my wife. But I never feared death afterwards. I've got no problem about dying. I know there's a happier place.

MAUD, FROM BELFAST, had an unusual experience while ill in bed with thyroid problems.

It happened in 1991. My mother had died in 1989 and I hadn't been well. I was still mourning for my mother. I hadn't mourned properly for her because my husband was taken into the hospital at the same time as she died. He was very ill and had a lot of things wrong. I wasn't well either with my thyroid. I didn't know that's what it was at the time but that's what it turned out to be.

I remember my face had broken out and I had lost a

massive amount of weight. I was in bed and wasn't feeling well at all. The doctor said to me, when he came into the room and saw my appearance, 'What has happened to you?' I still remember saying, 'Doctor, you know my mummy died.' He said, 'But that was two years ago.' There's always an expectation that there will be a change after a year or so but it doesn't happen like that. That's how I always know the exact year it happened.

I was very unsure about what was wrong with me. I thought it was something more serious. We all think of cancer, don't we? I remember doing tests up in the doctor's surgery. It was only six weeks until my son was getting married and I remember saying, 'Doctor, would you just keep me going for that length of time, until my son's wedding.'

The doctor looked at me and said, 'There is no cancer in your body.' He knew what I was thinking although I didn't say it. I thought I was going to die and I had just accepted it. But it transpired that my thyroid was underactive and that's what was wrong.

I don't know how long I was in bed. One night I was lying there and I had a strange experience. I was sleeping at the time. Suddenly there was a very bright light. There was an amazing brightness all over. It was just as if the whole place was lit up. There also seemed to be a tunnel, which was rounded. There was no black there, not even in the tunnel. Everything was white. I could see everything was very bright.

It was as if somebody was wheeling me along that tunnel. My body was lying on a stretcher and not a bed. I didn't see anybody doing the wheeling. They were at the head of the bed, pushing me, like you would see in a hospital. The bed clothes were white, like you would have in a hospital bed. I wasn't going fast. I was moving slowly.

It was as if I was seated up above and looking down at me

being wheeled along. I was about ceiling height, not away up in the sky or anything like that. I couldn't see my face but I knew it was me or thought it was me in the bed. I really didn't have to even think about it – that was me getting wheeled along.

I could see a curtain, like a thin lace curtain, at the end. It was moving slightly, as if there was a wee wind or a draught or something. I didn't see anything beyond it but it was like as if it was the outside. When I think of what was beyond it, to me it was just peace. But I didn't go through the curtain. Suddenly everything stopped. It just came to an end.

I know that when I wakened up in the morning it was as if peace had come over me. It was like I had a change of mind overnight. I thought to myself, 'What am I mourning my mother for?' She had been ill for years and I felt, 'I wouldn't want her back to suffer that again.' I could never have thought that way before about my mother. All of a sudden I asked, 'What am I worrying about?' I wouldn't say I stopped mourning for my mother, as a result, but I certainly stopped worrying.

I got well again quickly after that. By the time my son was married I was quite well. I had put on weight again. I think a lot of things changed for me after that. I don't think I ever worried the same about anything again. I also thought about what happened over the years. I remember saying about it to my son but I don't talk to other people about it. They would think something was wrong with you.

I have often heard since about similar experiences although I never knew anything about them before what happened to me. But it definitely happened. It's fresh in my mind to this day. And that was the start. That was the first day I felt in any way well. It was like as if there was peace there. It changed everything. It changed the way that I thought and it changed my life.

PADDY, FROM COUNTY WICKLOW, went through a medical procedure back in the 1980s which went badly wrong. What followed changed his life.

I had a pain in my chest and I went in for tests. You walk on a treadmill and all that sort of stuff. I had a small blockage. I was told by the cardiologist, 'You're very lucky because there's a new procedure coming in called angioplasty.' What happens is you go in and they photograph your veins and they can actually see where the blockage is.

They then put a tube in and push it right up through to the blockage and they press a button. It blows up and it clears the blockage away. You never have problems anymore. He said, 'You're ideal for it. You're in perfect nick, have a good heart, good everything.' They had only done a few of these procedures up to then.

I went in to have the operation, which I remember was scheduled for 14 February. I was there a few days beforehand so they could do all the tests. By a remarkable coincidence, when I got into the hospital the sister in charge of the ward started talking to me and we found out that her sister had been a friend of my wife. So we became close. She said, 'I've never seen the operation so I'll go in and watch it and I'll ring your wife as soon as it's over.'

Coming up to the operation I started writing a diary. But I couldn't do it anymore because I had a great foreboding the day or so before it. I felt something was going wrong. Things weren't helped by the arrival of a priest the night before to hear my confession and give me a blessing. He was the local parish priest. He turned out to be the brother of our next door neighbour. That was a terrible omen to me. I didn't feel good about it at all.

Come the operation, there were at least five guys around the table – anaesthetists, this, that and the other. I was under sedation although I was aware when they were doing it. They put the catheter in and pushed it up. Then they pressed the button and it didn't work. There was an explosion in my chest, like a heart attack. It wasn't supposed to happen. It was like putting something down a sink drain and it doesn't work. The pain was atrocious. I shouted because the pain was so bad. And I died!

I went out of my body. I was looking down from the ceiling. I saw them below me putting jump-leads on my chest to revive me. I was aware of the panic around although I was also aware that I wasn't part of it. The sister of the hospital ran out of the room and rang my wife and said, 'Everything has gone wrong.' She saw I had died. But I was totally separate from myself. It was like observing a scene, like watching television.

I saw a light and a tunnel. It was like the way a flame-thrower goes. The flames seemed to go in a circle, very fast, like a rocket ship. The nearest thing I could think of similar to it would be an upwards circular chimney. I felt I was being sucked up. Suddenly I asked, 'Do I continue or not? Should I stay or should I go?'

I seemed to have the right to stay or go. I was aware I had a choice. I felt that very much. I decided to stay although I firmly believe that if you want to go you can go. I said, 'No, I'm not leaving.' I suppose I wasn't ready to go. I had a young family and I'm a perennial optimist. I had more to do. So I decided to go back.

It must have been all over in seconds, in real life. They put me in Intensive Care. I was covered in drips and I couldn't move. It was very disquieting. The operation was a complete failure. It did nothing for me. Medically it did ten per cent damage to my heart but I never had any problems since. It transpired that they really shouldn't have done the procedure in the first place. There's a ten-year window and if you last the ten years then you're normal again. So I'm fine since. I'm still here.

In many ways the experience has been for the good. It didn't make me a saint or anything but I think it improved me. It gave me a chance to look at my life and my luck. It made me aware about spirituality and that if you don't have spirituality life is emptier. It sharpened my awareness. I tried to learn things afterwards rather than just assuming that you don't know everything. I tried to become less judgemental.

It changed my view about death. It made me much more comfortable about the idea of dying. I have less fear – not more courage, just less fear. I also think there has to be something afterwards. Historically, knowledge passes through the system. Things, like good and evil, permeate through the ages. They can be transferred on.

It's not a religious thing but there has to be more. Something of you definitely lives on. There is something bigger, something broader. There are powers beyond our brief existence. If you've done good or you've created love, that's sufficient to live on for a little bit. We definitely all leave a shadow in some shape or form.

CATHERINE, FROM DUBLIN, had an extraordinary near-death experience while in hospital to have her uterus removed.

It happened over 40 years ago. I had a total hysterectomy at the time. I had also complained of a pain in what the consultant called my 'kidney.' He said, 'Sure, while you are in, we will have a look at it.' In those days there was no rush to get rid of patients from hospital. He also knew I had five young kids so he said, 'I'll keep you in as long as I can.'

I had the hysterectomy on a Wednesday. On Thursday night a nurse came around and said, 'I have to give you an injection. It will help the radiologist get a clearer picture.' I said, 'Of what?' She said, 'Oh, the professor said we are to have a look at your kidney.' I said, 'I'm in no fit condition to have this. I've just had major surgery.' How and ever, she insisted.

The next morning I was brought up to the theatre. I was very feeble. I had to be brought up in a wheelchair and put on the surgical table. It was only going to be a normal procedure, nothing horrendous, and there weren't that many medical people there.

They then started to put something into the back of my hand. It was like a needle to inject some kind of a relaxant. I don't know what possessed me to think I was dying but I said, 'Please stop! I can't go through with this! I know I'm going to die!' I was pleading with them.

I just took off into a tunnel. It was more like a long tent. It was coloured cream, made of canvas and about six-foot wide. The tent was in segments, where there would be a frame maybe every six feet. It was sufficiently big for me to be in the middle of it. I was raised up, not really floating but elevated. I was still in the lying position although I didn't feel I was lying on anything. I could see ahead but I didn't seem to be moving. I was quite calm.

Down at the end of the tent there was a light. It was a 'brightness', like somebody was standing outside and shining a searchlight in. At the end of the tunnel was my mother, who had died. I don't know if you ever remember how, in my mother's or my grandmother's time, they would wear a

Foxford dressing-gown with the cord around the waist. Well, my mother had a red Foxford dressing-gown on.

My mother was calling me to her. She was saying, 'You are going to be alright!' Her cure for everything – even if you had a pain in your tummy – was a cup of warm water with a drop of pepper in it. She was at the kitchen door, at the end of this tent, telling me, 'Don't worry. I have the saucepan in my hand and this is going to cure you.'

My aunt then appeared behind her. She was dressed in a blue dressing-gown. She was my father's sister. She was the type of woman that, in those days, you could go and talk to. I would go and talk to her about my problems. She was saying, 'No, Kay! Go back!'

I think the choice was being left to me as to whether I was going to go with my mother or take my aunt's advice. I took it that if I had gone to my mother I would have died. But by obeying my aunt to go back I was going to live.

Throughout all this, there had been pandemonium in the theatre. They started to panic. Someone was shouting for this, that and the other. I remember a doctor was calling for ten milligrams of something. A nurse was saying, 'I haven't got ten milligrams.' He kind of rather rudely said, 'You stupid fool! Two fives make a ten and I want them immediately!' I could hear all this, as plain as anything. I could see the pandemonium but I was helpless and could do nothing about it. I could also see that my prediction about dying was right.

I suddenly went 'plonk' and I came back down into my body. I must have made a split-second decision, probably based on the fact that I had five young kids at home under the age of twelve. So I was obeying my aunt rather than my mother. She had made the decision for me and I had taken it. I was back.

I can't remember all that happened then because I only

woke up back in the ward. I don't remember being taken from the theatre to the ward. I didn't know until the next morning how bad things had been. A more senior nurse came on duty and she said to me, 'My God! I believe we nearly lost you yesterday.' That was the only reference that was made to what happened.

The funny thing about it, in hindsight, is that I never complained to the consultant about it. Maybe I was so glad that I had escaped. I had a sense of relief and I didn't bother complaining. I would tend to ask a lot of questions, even back then. I was on great terms with him and he had delivered my children. But I just didn't ask him.

I don't think too much about what happened. It's only now, as I get older, that I remember some of these things. Reminiscence is the privilege of the elderly! I would have thought I had imagined the whole thing except I read of other people and I realised it did occur. What happened certainly cured me of the fear of death. And I realise now that, all those years ago, I had the choice to stay or to go.

MICHAEL PATERSON was on patrol with the RUC in Belfast, in 1981, when his Land Rover was hit by a rocket-launched grenade. Badly injured, the 24-year-old was taken to hospital where he had a near-death experience. He eventually qualified as a psychologist.

Back in September 1981 I was on patrol with the RUC in Belfast. I had two-and-a-half years service at the time. I was married for three weeks and it was my wife's birthday. I had been posted to Belfast, on transfer, which facilitated married life. My wife worked in a job in Belfast and couldn't transfer elsewhere.

I was in West Belfast, on a two-vehicle mobile patrol. We

were travelling a street called the Suffolk Road. An RPG-7, which is a rocket-propelled grenade, was fired at my vehicle. It came through the driver's door and killed the driver. It amputated both my arms and smashed my left leg, before it burned through my door and exploded outside. Fortunately it didn't explode inside – otherwise I wouldn't be here to tell the tale.

There was an immediate loss of blood from my arms being severed and my femur being smashed. I had fog-like vision although I was still conscious. I was aware that the horns on the vehicle were going. My arm flying off must have hit the switch. I was sitting there for what seemed like a long time. I was aware that my right arm was amputated and that my left leg was smashed but I have no memory of what my left arm looked like.

I was conscious and I could speak OK but I was in a dissociated state. I wasn't feeling a lot of pain at that stage. Apparently we were under fire at the same time and the police in the second vehicle didn't get out. So I was there for quite a while, in relative terms. Eventually one of my colleagues opened the door and I looked out at him standing there. I said, 'Can you get me out?' He said, 'Sit there!' So I did. I wasn't going anywhere, anyway.

After a while two army medics arrived. One of them parcelled up my arms. A while later the ambulance crew arrived. They got me out of the Land Rover and into the ambulance. This was the sorest part because I could feel the pain in my left leg at this point. I was aware of the journey to the hospital. I kept my eyes closed. As the ambulance went around a corner I could feel myself pressing against the side of the cot I was on, and that was sore.

I also remember arriving at the hospital Accident and Emergency which was literally only a few minutes away. I was taken in and there was a lot of activity around me. Somebody contacted my wife. I remember it was quite strange because I was only married a few weeks and I wasn't used to the term 'wife' yet. They were putting drips in at this stage and I was aware of slipping into unconsciousness.

The incident occurred about half-ten in the morning, I think, and I must have been up in the operating theatre about half-eleven. They phoned up the theatre to say I was on my way and they cancelled the rest of the theatre list. Somewhere between half-eleven and six-thirty that night I had a near-death experience.

I was suddenly aware of being in a dark tunnel, with a light at the end of it. I was travelling along the tunnel and ending up in the white light. It felt as if I was standing up in the tunnel. I was aware of darkness or blackness on the walls and ceiling. It was like a Tube tunnel, like you see in the London Underground. It was that sort of shape. It felt like I was moving at a steady pace, drifting along. There was no sound, as far as I can remember. It was more of a sensual thing, a sense of peace.

I was aware of the bright light at the end of it. I was moving towards it. It was like a circle of light which got bigger as I got closer. I was moving along in the blackness and the next thing I was in the light itself. I'm not sure if that was the point of me actually dying. I said to the surgeon a number of years later, 'Tell me this, when I was in the theatre with you did I die?' He said, 'Why do you ask?' I explained to him why. He said, 'You did, but obviously we got you back.' So I was dead for a while.

My memory is that there were ghostly figures around me. They were in the white light itself. I couldn't see them until I was there. The features of the figures around me weren't clear. They were fog-like. They just blended in. If you can picture smoke or mist, and somebody's head and shoulders formed in it, that's what the figures were like. That's what I was aware of – head and shoulders. I wasn't looking any lower than that.

It was almost like people I knew but I couldn't say who the people were. I wasn't aware of anything being said to me but I felt very much at peace and felt very welcome. I felt very comfortable. It was extremely pleasant. It felt like these were friends or relatives but who they were I didn't know. When I was there it was like a spiritual experience. I felt very close to God. The thought that I was dying, or might die, had never crossed my mind when I was conscious before the experience happened.

I had a lot to live for. I was only married a few weeks. I was very physically fit. I felt good within myself, very positive about life. So when I was in the white light I thought, 'It's not right for me to be here.' I got a sense of, 'I don't belong here yet.' I didn't know I was dead but I felt, 'Thanks for the welcome but I'm not staying too long.' I don't know how I came back. It was like a sudden return. I think I was defibrillated and that might account for why I have no memory of going backwards or anything.

The next thing I remember was coming around in Intensive Care that night. It was about half-six. I could see my family around me. I knew my arms were off. I could look down and see the bandages and that confirmed it. I could see my leg in traction. When I was speaking to my family I described feeling very close to God. It was the only way I could describe what happened. My mother's aunt took it very literally and bought me a King James Bible. I didn't really mean it in that sense.

It was a spiritual experience but I didn't start going to church on a regular basis or anything like that. In some ways I would nearly question the purpose of organised religion. I have a belief in a 'higher being' but I'm uncomfortable with the way the higher being is worshipped by different people. One group says, 'Our way is the right way.' Others say, 'No, it's the wrong way; ours is the right way.' I think the 'greater being', whatever it is, is probably more than what humans understand at the moment.

I had never heard of the term 'near-death experience' before. I never knew of the bright lights. It was only a few years later, probably in 1983, when I was reading a psychology textbook I saw a feature on the near-death experience. I said, 'What's this near-death experience?' It described being in the 'dark tunnel' and the 'light at the end of the tunnel.' I read it with interest and thought, 'Oh! That happened to me. I've experienced that.'

I think back on it occasionally and say, 'That was an interesting experience, especially from the point of view that I went on to become a psychologist.' I have talked to clients who have been in traumatic situations and I have come across one or two over the years who have had experiences similar to mine. It's not the sort of thing I'd ask about. There could have been a lot more only I haven't asked.

But the topic can come up and there certainly can be similarities to me and I know where people are coming from. With a few people – especially when I've worked with clients who have a fear of death – I have sometimes shared the fact that I have been there and I was comfortable with it. It has been valuable to them.

I am certain the experience was real. I knew I had died at some point. The consultant knew too but nobody told me until later. It's a unique position I have been in. I still have that inner peace. And I have no fear of death. As a child I would have thought it would be a terrible thing to die. But, now that I've been there, it's alright. Whenever it comes to me, it will be

OK. The only sadness I would have would be leaving people behind that I love. Other than that, it's fine.

ALISON DAVIS, FROM COUNTY DUBLIN, saw bright lights and heard distant voices during her experience, which occurred while she was in hospital following a serious car crash.

One day I was out doing a message for my work. A colleague was driving the car and I was in the front passenger seat. He didn't know the roads but I did. We were coming to a crossroads and there was a stop sign. Trees grow there and to this day they are still growing over the stop sign. He didn't see it and I didn't think to remind him.

We went straight across and there was a lorry coming up the other way. The lorry went into the driver's side of us, coming in from the back. That's what I was told later because I didn't see anything at the time.

I was thrown completely forward and I went through the windscreen. Afterwards I learned that the gear stick went into my sternum. One of my eyes was protruding and full of blood. I was conscious but totally in shock. Other than that, the damage was all internal.

A church minister was talking to me although I didn't know it at the time. He was from a nearby church. He came along and saw what had happened and was praying over me. There was no ambulance available so a van that used to do all the deliveries with the bloods came out for me. I was put in it.

When I got to Casualty they were all around me saying, 'You'd better get your next of kin,' but I wasn't able to tell them anything. I was brought up to one of the wards and I can still remember the doctor and the nurse whose name was Geraldine Morrison. I was given an injection every couple of hours.

I welcomed the injections because there was so much pain. They didn't hurt because the pain was that bad. I was coming in and out of a coma at this stage. I was out of it half the time. There was little damage and, believe it or not, the only scar I have now is in my right eyebrow. But they were worried about internal bleeding.

All I kept seeing was this light. There was loads of light. The light was a pinkish-white. It was like a huge circle all around me. It was around the whole bed. If I looked right or left it was there. I can still see it to this day. The light was more pink than white and it was blinding.

There were no lights on in my room but I kept seeing it. I couldn't see anything beyond it. I was wondering, 'Where am I?' I was very conscious of it. It was there for a long time. I might fall back into a coma but when I would wake up it was still there, over my head.

I could also hear voices and I thought, 'I must be dead.' It was like the voices were saying prayers. They sounded like they were really far away and very gentle and soothing. They were trying to keep me calm, saying to me, 'There's no need to worry.'

The voices were saying, 'Do you think she is listening? Does she understand?' But I couldn't answer. It was as if I was paralysed and couldn't respond. I was thinking, 'What do they mean? What are they saying that I can't understand? I must be in another world.'

The next thing I could feel someone holding my hand and patting my head. It felt like a female hand because it was very soft. I could feel the hand on my head, stroking it and stroking my forehead. I thought when I looked through a haze that I could see a white, chiffon-like sleeve attached to this small, soft hand but I could never see a face. I felt the hand was lifting me up and I thought, 'I'm going up to that light now. They must be taking me with them.'

I felt I was travelling. I thought I was sailing somewhere. It felt like I was being gently steered in a lifting position. Eventually I opened my eyes and could see nobody. I rang for the nurse and she came in. I said, 'I think there were some people here, talking to me.' She said, 'There wasn't anybody here.' She said there was definitely nobody in. I said, 'I'm so sure there was.'

After a couple of days they realised that I had a collapsed lung. They had to drain off all the excess fluid. By the end of my second week I was getting better. The minister who had come to the scene of the accident came in to visit. He was very worried about me and couldn't get me off his mind.

I was telling him my experience. I was trying to explain to him what I had seen. I was saying, 'There was definitely somebody here but I don't know who it was.' He said, 'God must have been with you. Somebody was looking after you.' He also told me he had been there at the accident. He had been with me and had been praying with me.

I ended up being in hospital for a month. When I came out I was a totally different person. Later on, my mum died very suddenly and I remember the very last thing she said to me when she was alive in the hospital was, 'Please take me towards the light.' She kept saying it. I kept thinking she wanted to go towards the windows.

I came home and the hospital rang me to say she was dead. I wondered then was it only because I had told her what had happened to me. Or maybe she was experiencing it herself. I know whenever I see someone elderly who is dying now I say, 'You will be off in a lovely place with lots of nice people around you and all your friends and loads of lovely bright lights.'

I think back a lot on what happened and all the things that transpired. I can still visualise it to this day. It comes to me mostly when I am alone, maybe in the house at night when it is empty. They would be the times when I would dwell on it more. As you get older, maybe you dwell on things that happened in the past and you ask yourself, 'Why did they happen?'

I speak about it to almost nobody but I always pray to God and Padre Pio. I want to be in grace if something happens. I also feel there has to be a reason. We don't always know what that reason is and when we see the awful things that can happen to people – especially young people – it can be so hard to take. But there has to be a reason and maybe one day we will understand it.

I certainly know that I was being helped through that month and in particular through the very bad two weeks. Something was definitely looking after me and I don't know what it was. Seeing that light has given me hope and tells me there is more. It makes me feel that there is something there when I eventually pass away.

FRANCES, FROM COUNTY LIMERICK, describes what happened during a childbirth that went badly wrong.

I had my baby back in 1969. The baby was fine but I got very sick. I didn't know what was happening to me. I had a haemorrhage. They didn't really know what caused it. They could never figure it out. I don't remember the childbirth. I don't remember my husband coming in. I can't recall a single thing. Eventually I was shifted from the nursing home to the hospital. I was there for a month or so.

The only time I came around the tiniest bit was when they were wheeling me into the hospital. I was on a trolley and it banged off something. One guy started arguing with the other guy who was after banging the trolley. He was saying, 'My God! What are you after doing!' I woke up with that bang and I said, 'Don't be fighting over it. It's OK.' The only other time I woke up a bit was in the theatre, where they were operating to try and stop the haemorrhaging. I don't remember anything else after that.

At some stage, back in my hospital bed, I left my body. I was above, probably a little higher than the ceiling. I just took off and floated along. I could see myself lying on the bed, clear as anything. I can remember seeing the nurse down below, holding onto my wrist. She was standing there with the doctor. They were both looking at me on the bed. The nurse looked up at the doctor and said, 'She's gone!' I was above them when she was saying this. I was definitely looking down at them and I wasn't there on the bed.

I was floating along as if to a sunset or a sunrise. I couldn't say which one of them it was. It was just beautiful. The sunrise or sunset was at the end of what might have been a tunnel but I'm not sure. It certainly was some kind of 'space'. I could see the light at the end, in the distance. I was floating towards it. I was happy and it was really nice. There was nothing frightening.

I then turned around and I saw what I thought was the image of Our Lady behind me. It was her outline. I didn't see her face. I couldn't make out her clothes. It was just the dark grey outline of what was like an old-fashioned nun. But I knew that it was her. I automatically knew it.

She was where I had come from. She was just standing there, on the level of the ground, but I was on top floating. I wondered how I could have passed her out without seeing her. Her hands came up out in front of her and it was as if she was indicating to me to come back. Her elbows were on her ribs and her hands were spread out and being brought back into her chest nice and gently. They were sort of waving me back. I turned back and then I was OK. It had all lasted for about a minute.

I remember no more for a long time after that. I couldn't tell you how long. I was eventually discharged. Later on I learned that I had almost died. I remember meeting the consultant and he picked up the edge of a piece of paper that you write a prescription on. He said, 'That's how near you were to being dead!' I got a shock over that. But I never told him what I should have told him – 'I know I was dead!' Back in those days you didn't talk up to doctors.

I have thought about it loads of times over the years. I have only said it to a couple of people and that was years and years later. I was too embarrassed. I wouldn't say it to very many – only to one of my sisters and people like that. They would say, 'You should tell someone.' But who would I be telling? They'd be thinking I was crazy.

I'd think about it if I read about a near-death experience. I'd say, 'I think I had that kind of experience as well.' When something like it would come up, I would say, 'I wonder are they going to describe my one? I wonder will anybody else have had one similar to mine?' But, no matter what I read, I never came across exactly the same as what happened to me.

JEREMY O'NEILL, FROM COUNTY KERRY, **experienced some elements, but not all, of a near-death journey, including the out-of-body travel, seeing an intensely bright light and meeting with a deceased family member.**

In the evening, after work, I often go home and lie down in the bedroom and just relax for a while. One evening, in early 2009, at a quarter past six, I was lying in the bed and I sort of dozed off. All of a sudden I was out in what seemed like Muckross Abbey in Killarney. It's an old stone ruin in the National Park. There is an old church there and I was inside in a room which was down at the back of the church. You can imagine it – empty, with old stone walls.

I was looking through a stone window, up through the church. There were two Americans next to me and I was telling them, 'Right at the very back, at the opposite end, that's where the altar used to be.' That was the last I saw of the Americans.

All of a sudden I saw this massive, blinding light right at the very back of the church, where the altar would normally be. It was like a circular light. You can imagine a very strong beam coming straight into your eyes. I kept staring and staring at this light. It got brighter and brighter. It enveloped my whole self.

I was lifted off the ground. I couldn't control myself. I was being lifted right up in the air, with my body horizontal to the ground. The next thing it was like I was flying down this street. I was looking at all the houses. It was like as if you were driving down a street in a car, looking at all the houses and the shops which were back in the time of maybe the 1960s or the '70s. You could compare it to driving up a street, with a camera on your car, and you kept seeing the shots of the buildings one after another. It was like passing through time.

I felt calm and at peace although I was moving fairly rapidly. I could see all the buildings as I was passing by. I passed a church and after that there was a pub. I could see my father's face, just his side face, looking sideways. He is dead now since 1971. I saw his side face exactly as it was, as if he was walking into a pub, as he would have done back at that time. I saw the side locks he used to have. It was so vivid, so real. He was the last thing I saw.

After that I was back again in this room at the back of the church and I knew I had to get out of there. I was weak and everything was dark. It was empty. I had to find a door. I got up and went over to the corner and reached this door. I opened it. Then I woke up. I sat up in the bed. It was 25-past-six. I remember the time because I looked at my watch. It was ten minutes exactly since I had got into the bed.

I called my daughter straight away. I said, 'Jesus Christ! I'm after having this strange experience!' I told her about it then. I felt a little bit frightened and wondered, 'What is this thing?' I also told my girlfriend later on.

At the start I wondered was it some sort of sign or some sort of near-death experience. It wasn't that I was ill. I wasn't unwell although I am on tablets for blood pressure – but half the country is on them. I wasn't well back in the '80s, when I had an operation, but that's a long time ago.

It hasn't changed my life at all although it certainly was something significant. It also wasn't a dream. I am positive of that. It's hard to explain why but it just wasn't. It was so real. I'm not the kind of person that believes in that kind of stuff. I'm not into that kind of thing. And I don't think there was any religious significance to it. But it definitely was the most unusual experience I ever had in my life.

ANN, WHO COMES FROM BRAY, COUNTY WICKLOW **but who lives in the UK, had a near-death experience while in hospital with heart problems. The event happened shortly after the death of her sister.**

My sister died a few years ago. She died of a stroke. She was 71 and had a family of 11 children. They all took it badly. It was a tragedy. I came back to Bray when I heard she was sick. I came back three times and I was there with her at the very end, when she died. She was the first one to die in my family.

Not long afterwards I collapsed with a heart attack. I was having my dinner with my husband. I said to him, 'There is something happening to me. I don't know what it is.' We came into the lounge and he put me onto the settee and he rang the ambulance. Strangely I had no pain. The hospital is only about six miles away. I was taken there and they said I had a silent heart attack, where you have no pain or no warning.

The hospital did all sorts of tests. They discovered that my heart was skipping a beat. To be truthful, I had known for a long time that there was something not quite right. I would get out of breath even though I didn't drink or smoke. Eventually they diagnosed me as having atrial fibrillation, which causes a fast and erratic heartbeat.

I was in a small ward in the hospital, not in Intensive Care. It had six beds – three on one side and three on the other. I was lying back in my bed, in the middle of one of the nights. The lights were on, as they always are in a hospital. I could see every other bed and I could see the nurses' station.

Suddenly I was in this tunnel. The tunnel was coloured blue. It was a nice blue. There was nothing else in it. It was just plain. It was like going through the tunnel from Liverpool to Ellesmere Port, which we use all the time. It was like that but had a light-blue colour instead.

I saw Maureen – my sister that died – running up this brightly-lit tunnel. I was running after her. It was my real self. It wasn't that I could just see myself as in a dream. It was really me who was doing the running. She wasn't very far ahead of me although she wasn't near enough for me to touch. I was shouting, 'Maureen! Wait for me!' She hadn't run in years – she was the eldest of us. I kept running after her. I continued to shout, 'Maureen! Maureen! Wait!'

She was dressed in her ordinary clothes and she looked the same age as she was when she died. She never said anything. She just kept waving her hand back at me as if to tell me to go away. She faintly looked back once but it was mostly her hand that she was waving. I can still see her doing it now.

She was running towards a light at the end of this tunnel. The light was at the other side of the ward. It was really bright, like a very nice sunny day. I don't know if she ever made it to the light. I certainly didn't because I suddenly woke up with a shock. My heart was pounding. She was gone. The tunnel disappeared. It all just went. The whole thing had lasted for probably about a minute.

I woke up crying and I was upset. I realised immediately that the tunnel was gone. I saw that the tunnel had been a little bit to the right of me, between my bed and the opposite wall. There was actually a bed where it was. I saw that when I came to and focused.

I was very upset for weeks after. I was demented thinking about it. I couldn't figure out what had happened and why my sister had been running away. I couldn't understand why she didn't wait for me. I was disappointed because she didn't stop. I wanted to follow her and go to the light.

I never told the doctors. However, I did tell several people, including my family, and some just laughed. They said, 'It was the medication you were on.' I also told a priest, who was a friend of mine, and he said, 'That was God telling your sister to tell you he didn't want you yet.' He said, 'God obviously has plenty of good work for you to do.'

Initially I thought it was a dream but I have thought since that maybe I was dying. Yet I still don't know what it was. I have read about similar things in books and laughed. I thought people only imagined things like that. It frightened me in a way but not as much as I'd expect it to frighten me. It also brought back my sister's death. Mind you, I'm glad my sister didn't wait for me. And I know now that I will definitely meet her again.

SARAH, FROM COUNTY DONEGAL, had her experience when she was aged 43 and undergoing an operation in hospital. Two of the classic near-death elements feature in her story – journeying out of her body and a meeting with people from the other side.

I was coming out of the operation for a hysterectomy in the local hospital. I was in hospital for a long time but I was only in for a long time because my bladder wouldn't work afterwards. Otherwise it was a very ordinary procedure, not terribly long, relatively routine.

After the operation I was being revived by the nurses. They were trying to bring me around but I was up on a height, up on a different plane. I was up just about as high as a room, maybe eight feet or so above them. I could see the hospital bed below and I could see myself lying on it. I could make myself out clearly. I knew it was me yet I was up above. I could see that the white of the sheets was a kind of a grey compared to the white I could see up where I was.

I could also see two nurses trying to waken me up. They had their uniforms on them and they were giving me pats on the face. I could see them plainly. I could see what they were doing to me but I couldn't feel it. I was separate from myself.

Three people were coming towards me. They were very old and in human form. They were straight and tall and they all wore thin, long, white, gleaming garments. They had white, pale skin with very long, white, gleaming hair. Everything was very white on them. They were quiet and serene. They weren't recognisable to me and I couldn't tell what sex they were. Yet they had three different faces.

I didn't know them and I couldn't say that they were anybody in particular. They definitely weren't my grandparents because I knew them – unless this was the body they have in the next world. The background that they were coming from was something like a wood area, with trees or something of that nature. There was something like greenery behind them. There were no houses, just a kind of a soft background. Their arms weren't outstretched but I knew for a fact that their purpose was to come for me.

I was trying to get to them before the nurses got me wakened. I could see the nurses down below, hitting me and trying to get me to come around. I knew that if they got me wakened I wouldn't get to these people. I was aware of that. I was so anxious to go to them and I didn't want to come back.

I wanted to go to them as if they were long-lost relatives or ancestors or friends or something. It was an overwhelming desire. I definitely felt a great empathy with them. I felt they were my kindred. I felt akin to them, if there is such a thing. It was an extraordinary feeling.

Then I wakened up and the nurses were saying, 'Oh! We had bother getting you awake, bringing you around.' I was kind of annoyed and said, 'But I didn't want to come back!' I wanted to go to this fabulous place where there was such a great feeling. I wanted to get to these people.

It was like when you waken from a dream. When you waken from it, it's gone and you can't get it back again but you'd love to. Like, my husband is dead and sometimes I would dream about him and I would like to get it back again. But you can't.

That was how I came out of the operation. It was a lovely

experience and I kind of felt that if I had died then it would be a lovely thing. I am not scared of death since. I believe there's another world. And I feel that maybe that's what it's going to be like when I pass away.

I haven't really given what happened much thought in the last years. It's not the sort of thing that comes up in conversation very often. But if anybody is talking about after-death experiences, I will always say, 'Oh, I had one of them!'

NUALA, FROM DUBLIN, outlines what happened to her while pregnant when living in London.

My experience happened a good few years ago, when I was about 22. I'm in my 70s now. I was eight months pregnant at the time and was attending a clinic. I was prescribed medication. There was another woman there who already had her baby and she was being given afterbirth medication. Unfortunately a staff nurse got the medication mixed up and she gave me the afterbirth tablets.

I got very ill. I was doubled up in pain. I started to shiver and I got bloated. It was a while before they spotted the problem. The poison had gone through my whole system. I ended up being anointed twice. It was a case of life or death. Unfortunately the child – a boy who was baptised Seán – died having lived for an hour. Both my husband and I were very upset.

At one stage, while I was out of it, the doctors were beside me at my bed when I suddenly went through darkness like a tunnel. I was travelling. It seemed I was moving pretty fast. Then I came from the blackness into a large area where there was a lovely brightness. It was like a most unusual sky, coloured blue. It was the most beautiful blue you ever saw, very light in colour, even lighter than sky blue. The brightness was fantastic.

I was being met by a figure bringing me up into the light. The figure was coming towards me. It was a figure in garments, with the hands outstretched. The garments were all lovely bright colours. He was coming for me. I knew that because he had his arms out to grasp me. I knew it was Jesus and, much later on, I recognised from a picture that it was like the Divine Mercy, with the hands out.

The blue sky was behind him. There was someone else there in the background but I wasn't able to recognise who it was. The figure in the front seemed gentle and lovely but I didn't want to go. I asked him not to take me yet. I told him there were some things I hadn't finished doing. I didn't have any other children but I think, at the back of my mind, I was concerned for my mother.

While this was happening there were a lot of doctors talking about my condition. I could hear everything they were saying. As far as I could make out, they thought I was pretty well dead at the time. They thought I was gone. They were making plans for my mother and family to come over from Ireland. They didn't know that I could hear all this going on.

Eventually the figure went back further and further, as if on a treadmill. I then came back. I actually sat up in the bed. The doctors were delighted. They must have got the shock of their lives when they saw me sit up. I felt better immediately. The staff brought in this gorgeous dinner. I ate every bit of it.

Then I got bad again. My body was paralysed. I couldn't speak to anyone. I could only communicate with my index finger. If I raised my index finger twice I meant 'No'. If I raised it three times I meant 'Yes'. It was the only finger I could use. Within the next week I seemed to be worse and I was anointed again.

I was six weeks on my death-bed, during which I had yet another near-death experience. Eventually I was sent for several weeks of convalescence. When I was leaving, the cook came up and got down on her two knees in front of me and she said, 'Bless me, child! You've been very ill and you're a miracle!'

One of the doctors told me I had been near-dead. Another one told me, 'You know, you left us twice.' That same doctor was so overwhelmed by what had happened to me, and how I miraculously came back twice, that himself, his wife and his six children all converted to Catholicism.

The experience changed me forever. I think that before it happened I used to be a better Catholic but I am now a better Christian. If anyone said anything about the Catholic Church I'd have eaten the head off them. I'd have never seen their point of view. I thought I was a great Catholic doing that – being on the defensive all the time. But, after what happened, I wanted to help people and I wasn't like that before.

I have had a lot of rocky roads since then but I came through them all. And I have never forgotten what happened. I used to worry, years ago, when I'd see a priest going into a house to give someone the last rites. I now think, 'The person who is dying is lucky. They are seeing heaven. They are now getting a preview of it before they go.'

JANE SMYTH, FROM COUNTY WICKLOW, **had a stroke and a near-death experience after giving birth to a child in the National Maternity Hospital in Holles Street, Dublin.**

I was in Holles Street and I had a new baby. I was sitting in the bed, waiting for my husband to come in, when a clot went to the brain. I felt something travelling to my head. It was like it was rushing there. I had a massive stroke. I died, they told me afterwards.

I went towards this bright light. It was a beautiful white light. It didn't blind me or anything. I was floating along and I wasn't worried. When I got to the end I was in a place that was magnificent. It had a little stream in the middle and green grass on both sides of the stream. It wasn't a huge river or anything. It was lovely. It was so peaceful. The peace was wonderful.

There was this lovely bridge – a wicker bridge, interwoven, with the wicker going in and out. When I looked at it Our Lord was standing at the top of the bridge. He was dressed all in white. He had long black hair, shoulder-length. He was beautiful. He had his hand up and he was calling me. He was saying, 'Come on!'

He wanted me to go. I was saying to him, 'No. I can't go yet. If I go now, if I cross that bridge, I'm gone. I'll never see my family or my new baby again. I can't go over that bridge. I can't cross it yet.' I was thinking I had my little baby at home. I said, 'No. I'm not going because of my little baby at home.'

I could see my granny there. I knew her the minute I saw her. She was in a beautiful little cottage with roses all around it. She was cutting the roses off the bushes. It was by the stream. She was on the left-hand side of the stream. She said to me, 'What are you doing here? You shouldn't be here.' With that, Our Lord gave me a choice as to whether I would stay or go. I knew if I crossed the bridge I was gone. I said, 'No. I can't cross that bridge, I'm not ready yet.' So I started to come back.

They rushed me from Holles Street to the Mater and they put me on all these life-support machines and gave me injections into the spine. They brought me back and they told me I was after dying. They didn't say for how long but that my heart had stopped. They told me I was lucky to survive. Looking back, I suppose I had my choice – to go or to come back. But I am glad I came back and I recall what happened as an incredible experience.

ANNI DIXON had her experience while undergoing surgery following an ectopic pregnancy. She was living at the time on the West Cork/Kerry border.

I had an ectopic pregnancy where the fallopian tube ruptured six days before they took me to hospital. You can die within a half-hour of a ruptured fallopian tube because you are bleeding internally. I had reached the point where I was fainting when I was sitting up. If I got up, there were huge, great clots of blood coming out. I was within a thread of losing my life.

I was on the brink of death. I could feel it myself. I was bleeding to death. I felt my life's strength ebbing away. Everything became weaker. There was no strength in my muscles and there was no strength in my brain. My brain was sinking down. It was an unbearable effort to think. My life-force was just draining away from me.

They operated on me within 24 hours. I was under anaesthetic when I had this life-changing experience. There was an extraordinary rushing sensation, like rushing wind. It was all very black. There wasn't light, as people speak of when they talk about their near-death experiences. But the darkness and the rushing sense were inconsequential really. Instead there was a feeling of something enduring that never ends.

I had this awareness of an enormous consciousness of which mine was a part. My consciousness was released from its bodily form. The bodily form was completely insignificant.

It was like a drop in the ocean and part of something much, much bigger. I had this distinct sense that it could reach anywhere. There was this feeling of reaching across space.

I was aware that this consciousness is present in all material forms. Whether it is plants or animals, or human forms, or rock forms, doesn't really make any difference. All of those forms are not separate. The overpowering thing was this great sense of life which was happy and joyous, this wonderful sense of abundant, extraordinary creativity.

There was a sense that the body was like a leaf that could be shed in the fall and had no greater significance than that. The body is simply a particular construction of material atoms. The meaning that was conveyed was to let the bodily form just flow away. There is something much more enduring that never ends, which is totally bigger. It's incomparable and a different dimension.

There was also a sense that to experience life is a gift, no matter what the circumstances. It doesn't matter how difficult our life experiences are, they are that way for a reason. And they are a gift, no matter how destructive and painful they seem to be. The core communication that was being conveyed was that life itself is vital, it's there forever, it's indestructible, it's playful, joyous and humorous. That was very fruitful for me, personally, because I felt very overwhelmed by my life circumstances.

The whole thing may have only lasted seconds. It may have been a split second, because in the dimension of consciousness time does not work in the way we experience it in normal day-to-day life. I felt it was profound meaning that was being revealed. It was a revelation. It all felt very real. It was an experience that was given to me. That's what it felt like.

Afterwards my mind couldn't think of anything else. It changed my awareness of the fundamental meaning of life and that led to a whole range of insights. I came to understand that reincarnation is truly what happens. Bodies fall away but the intelligence remains and grows and develops. The consciousness of the individual constantly recycles because the individual is part of the whole.

I knew afterwards that there is a God. I had sensed the reality of God since I was a small child. I grew up in an atheistic, agnostic family, which insisted that God can only exist if it's scientifically proven. That was a terrible dilemma for me. All through my education I tried to talk to people about God but the people I met didn't want to talk about those kinds of things when I was growing up. So I just felt like a fool. I felt I must be wrong.

But when I had this experience I felt, 'I was right. It was right to trust my senses. God is real and this is God revealing himself to me.' It wasn't important after that to talk to anybody else about it or to get anybody else to believe what I saw. What was important was that I had this experience and that was enough for me.

That incident was important to my whole life. I came back out of this extraordinary space I'd been in, into the world I'd left, and I had changed but nothing else had changed. It wasn't that my life became easier but the experience gave me an awareness that helped me to make sense of things. It led me to a very different approach to my life.

It led me to try to be more tolerant, to act with integrity and to try to live very much by the teachings of Christ. It also led me to study about religion. Really the teachings of Christ are guidelines for living and that became a very real, tangible source to turn to when I was in doubt. It led me to try and find a religious discipline that I would find acceptable and that I could study in depth. It was totally life-changing.

MARY-ANN MURPHY, FROM CAHERSIVEEN, COUNTY KERRY, describes how her brother Kevin H. Murphy died in 1999, about two months after experiencing travel through a tunnel.

My brother Kevin was only 24 years old when he died. He was a very bubbly person but he was getting blackouts. It was discovered that he had a lung condition, which was diagnosed nine months before he died. It was diagnosed on the day of his birthday, 24 April 1998. He had pulmonary hypertension, which is high blood pressure of the lung. It plays on the heart and can eventually wear you out. We were hoping for a miracle and I prayed for one every day.

Towards the end, he was getting very breathless. He got a few attacks of breathlessness where he thought he was gone. One time, around early November, he had an attack which was like a bad faint. He was on his way to the bathroom from the bedroom. The next thing he collapsed. It all lasted about three minutes. Mammy thought he was gone, that he had died. She sat him on a chair and she held him in her arms.

When he came out of the attack, he told my mother that he had been in a tunnel. He had gone through this tunnel and it was a lovely, beautiful experience. He said it was a very comfortable feeling. He said it was very peaceful and that he wouldn't have minded going all the way. Mammy believed him. He seemed to be very happy to be going and he said it was wonderful. He was sure he was gone.

He felt very calm. He was ready to die. He was happy that if he died he was going to a better place. I think he told everyone about what had happened. I thought, 'Isn't it lovely to hear he had been to the other side. We will all have to go there sometime.' He had great acceptance.

People couldn't understand how a young man, with so

much to live for, could have such acceptance of going to the next world. He told a very good friend of his, 'You know, I'm going to die.' She said, 'Ah, Kevin, you won't.' He said he knew he was but he added, 'I'm not worried at all about myself but I'm very worried about my parents.'

I also remember going to visit him one day and I was crying because he wasn't well. I used to cry a lot because I thought, 'What am I going to do without him? I love him so much.' He said to me, 'It is me that should be crying!' He was always really bright and jolly. Yet I was the one crying because he was very weak that particular day.

He didn't tell me he was going to die until the day it happened. He said it straight out to me, 'I'm going to die!' I started crying. I didn't believe it. He was always very strong and wasn't a weak, sick person. I was still waiting for the miracle. I thought, 'He is too good for this to happen.' He was also due to go to England, where he hoped to get a transplant.

That Saturday evening I left him and went home. A man who goes around with the Legion of Mary and has a statue of Our Lady sat and prayed with him in the hospital. A priest went in to say a prayer over him too. Kevin told the priest, 'There is no need to pray for me. Just pray for my parents, for acceptance.'

Later he told the nurses, 'I'm going to die. Hold my hand.' One of them said she couldn't because it was too much for her. But another one held his hand. He got heart attack after heart attack and he died. He died on 31 January 1999.

I was later told by the man who prayed with him, 'Your brother is in heaven. I have only seen two people that were really happy about dying. Kevin was one and there was another elderly lady.' We often discussed how he felt that night. And I always tell people who are dying about Kevin's experience and I tell them not to be afraid.

SHEILA, whose 47-year-old husband Shaun died from cancer, describes his final hours and his passage to the other side. Although living in the UK, Shaun's father came from Downpatrick and Sheila's grandmother came from Galway. Their sons Matt and Stuart were present at the death.

Shaun was very restless. He was calling out, still in his child-hood, certainly not with us, with very loud breathing and mental anguish. We knew the end was coming. We could see the signs. At one point both Matt and I held him and told him that it was alright for him to go. There was no point in us trying to hold onto him. We had to let him go. He was not aware that we were there.

All I could do now for Shaun really was to wet his lips occasionally with water. He was incapable of eating or drinking and he was plagued with these terrible hiccups, which looked as though they hurt although I don't suppose they did. I was told that they were due to the movement of the diaphragm.

Later on Shaun's breathing changed. I called the boys, feeling slightly apprehensive because I wasn't sure how the end would be. Would it be violent and bloody? Or would it be peaceful? Anyway the boys had a right to be there if they wished and at this stage I thought that we probably only had a few minutes left. Instead we had over an hour of real peace.

We were blessed. We knew that 'they' were talking to Shaun and occasionally through Shaun's muttered conversations we could clearly hear what he said. At one point Shaun said, 'Am I coming back?' Then we heard him say a little later, 'I'll go over here, then.' This was not a figment of my imagination. All three of us heard the same things and we were sitting in different positions around the bed. The boys all heard it as well. We just looked at each other.

Shaun looked so peaceful, propped up on the pillows, resting on one elbow, with his eyes open for the first time in more than 24 hours, just looking upwards into the distance. I felt I couldn't say anything to him for fear of interrupting this lovely conversation he was having. It seemed to bring him great peace. I just held his hand.

I would have been intruding on something so very personal and private to him. Yet, in a way, probably without knowing it, he was sharing it with us. At one point Matt had held his other hand and said, 'I love you, Dad.' Shaun had whispered a reply – again, one that we all heard – 'I love you all too.'

About 20 minutes before he finally died, Shaun's face suddenly lit up. He had the look that a person has on their face when they suddenly see someone they haven't seen for years. How do you describe it? It was joy, happiness and recognition all rolled into one. His voice also held all three of these emotions as he said, 'Our Father' and then 'Hail Mary.' We all heard this conversation. The tone of voice had wonderment, reverence and love. And he had this look on his face.

We looked at each other and repeated what Shaun had said. I don't think any of us could quite believe it. I know, at the time, we actually thought he was seeing something, he was talking to someone. Someone else would say to you, 'It was the morphine.' It could well be, of course. I don't know. You would think afterwards it was a figment of the imagination but at the time it gave us great strength. From the things he was saying and the look on his face, it must have been a nice experience for him.

We knew that it was time for him to go, because he had suffered too much. We knew that Shaun was in heaven even though he breathed on very shallowly for another 20 minutes. I knew that I'd lost something tremendous. But we were really blessed to have witnessed this. It was a miracle and a gift from God to us.

No one can ever remove these memories from any of us. They will stay with us forever. I will never forget it. It left me with very strong faith and belief. I've always had belief in the afterlife. I always knew that there is something. To me, purgatory is the time you spend on earth. That's why I knew he was OK where he was going, because he was a good man. It has reinforced my own views. It is the legacy left to us which will hold us forever.

PAT LYNCH, FROM COUNTY LIMERICK, tells how a close friend had a near-death experience after suffering a heart attack while on holidays in County Clare.

I had a friend, Tom, who I met through playing soccer. He was a very popular fellow. He played up to the age of 40 and he was as good then as he was at 20. He always kept himself fit. He didn't drink or smoke, to my knowledge. He was also the most genuine and truthful man you could ever meet in your life.

He was working in the office of a factory in Shannon and I became production foreman there. We were there together for about 15 years. We also had been in the choir at St. John's Cathedral during the early years of our lives. There was an ongoing relationship there. We were close.

I remember he told me a story after he was retired from work. He would have been about 50 years old. He said he had been down playing golf in Kilkee, where he was on holidays with his wife. Kilkee is the 'Spain' to most people in Limerick. It's only about 60 miles away and a short drive.

He was playing golf when suddenly he got a heart attack. I don't know why they didn't bring him to the hospital in Ennis. Instead he was brought back to Barrington's Hospital in Limerick, by ambulance. They phoned in advance and everything was ready for his arrival – the equipment and the doctors.

He told me that he passed out inside in the hospital. He could remember distinctly floating over the bed. He could see the doctors working on him below. He could clearly remember his wife getting tangled in one of the leads attached to the machines. There was confusion. The next thing he could hear the doctors saying, 'He's gone! He's gone! He's gone!'

At that point, he said, he floated down what was like a corridor. At the end of it was what he described as a massive setting sun, like you would see over Galway Bay. It reminded him of the sort of setting sun where you would say to yourself, 'It's good to be alive!' He said there was a massive drive for him to get to it. The light was drawing him although he was going to it anyway.

Then, straight up in front of him, out of nowhere, his father appeared. He was dead for 30 years and had died of cancer. Back in those days, when his father had died, they had known very little about cancer and had very primitive treatments for it. They didn't have the drugs they have today. My friend said he died a worn man, drawn, with nothing left of him and his face shrivelled.

During my friend's heart attack, however, his father was like a man of 20. He said he never saw him in his life so good. His face was beautiful and fresh. His father put his arms out and embraced him. He called out his son's name, 'Tom!' He then said, 'Your time isn't up yet. You've got to go back.'

No sooner had he said that than he was back again,

hearing human beings. He could hear the doctor saying, 'We have him! We have him! Keep it up!' My friend was saying at the same time, 'Dad, don't leave me! Dad, don't leave me!' He was a bit embarrassed about it when he came to himself later on.

He told me that, as a result of what had happened, he would never again be afraid of death. That told me that it must have been a very pleasant experience. He died about eight years afterwards.

My own opinion is that while older people had no degrees in theology, they were God-gifted with a lot of common sense. You would often hear them saying, 'The light of heaven to you!' Christ was always the source of light. Darkness was the symbol of evil. There was always emphasis on light. It's my view that my friend saw the light of heaven. I am certain of it. I am convinced.

Unfortunately there are people today who are afraid to die. Everyone wants to get to heaven but by dying is the only way we can get there. We all have a fear of death. To me this is very concrete proof of what happens after death, coming from someone I loved in life, who wouldn't tell lies. It proves to me that there is a life hereafter. And I would totally stand on oath that what he told me that day was the absolute truth.

ETHNA, WHO COMES ORIGINALLY FROM COUNTY CORK but who now lives in Dublin, recalls a dying friend whose deceased husband called her to the other side.

I went in to see her in the hospital. She used to be gazing into space and lying in the hospital bed very ill. She had cancer and she was in her late 80s. She was just inside the door of the ward, with a curtain around her. She used to look as if she was waiting to move on and had lost all hope. I tried to cheer her up even though I knew I was wasting my time. I was saying, 'You'll be home soon.' She used to say, 'No, I won't. I don't want to go home.'

One day she said to me, 'My husband is waiting for me.' I thought she was hallucinating. He was dead ten years, or so, at the time. He had died from emphysema. They had been very close and idolised each other and she really missed him. I didn't want to say he was dead so I just asked her, 'What do you mean?' She said, 'I've been talking to him.' She told me he was down this tunnel which had flowers in it. Her husband was standing there and he said, 'I'm waiting for you. You've been long enough away.'

She was very specific when she spoke of the tunnel. It was when she mentioned it that I believed her. My husband was with me and he heard her too. She said it was a long tunnel and her husband was at the end of it. He was waving to her, calling her, beckoning her, it seems. She was looking straight at him.

Prior to that I thought she might have only been wishing to die. She had nothing much to live for and she didn't want to go home. But she was sure of what happened – her husband stood there and he was waiting for her and she couldn't wait to see him.

She was very sound of mind when she said it, and very lucid. There was no rambling. She then said to me, 'I just want to die. I wish I could go now. I don't know why I'm here.' She was livid that she had to live any longer. I said, 'It has been a long time on your own, hasn't it?' And she said, 'Too long.'

She knew she was going home. She said she would meet her other family there as well. She was smiling as she waited to move on. She wanted her body to give up and go. She really gave up after that and she died about three or four days later.

I definitely believe that my friend saw her husband in a tunnel. I believed her at the time and I still do. Maybe he came back as he was unhappy leaving because he didn't want to go without his wife. Whatever the reason, I know she really did see him. I know he was there waiting. And I will never forget her happiness that she was going to meet him again.

BERNIE, FROM COUNTY CORK, who has been a nurse all her life, describes how near-death experiences are commonly witnessed by medical staff.

The first story is one I came across myself. One morning I came on day duty. I was a surgical nurse, looking after post-op patients. They could be quite ill. They could have come in after accidents. There would be a few medical patients on the ward too. You could come on duty and meet up with any situation.

This particular day I was to look after a lady who was very weak, very unwell. She was bleeding and her blood pressure was way down. She was in shock and was unconscious throughout the morning. She wasn't aware of what was happening and she wasn't responding. They didn't think she would survive.

At about one o'clock she suddenly opened up her eyes. She said to me straight away, 'Oh, my God! I just met my mother!' She told me how her mother had put her hand up and said to go back, that her time wasn't right. She described her mother and said, 'She was exactly what she used to look like.' She was so pleased and said she had been talking to her in the same way that she was talking to me. I was dumb-founded.

I absolutely believed her. She was so clear in what she was telling me. I knew her because I had nursed her beforehand. I knew she was 'with it' and not off the rails or anything like that. To me she definitely saw her mother and she told her to go back, that her time wasn't up. I went off duty and that woman recovered. She lived for a further three or four years.

There was another person, a man who I was nursing at one stage. He was aged around 49. He had very bad circulation and wasn't very healthy. He was a very quiet man and he wouldn't talk to anyone, not even a nurse. He would cover his head, he was so shy. He was eventually sent to Intensive Care. Of the four people in there, he would have been the best. The others were very unwell.

My friend, who is a very good nurse, was working there at the time. She noticed how quiet he was. She also told me that, all of a sudden, he raised his head up and seemed to be looking at something. The next thing he was calling on different people he was seeing. He mentioned a load of names. He was saying, 'It's a beautiful place.' Then he would go back to being quiet again and he'd cover his head once more. This happened over and over again.

My friend told me that it was only when he started calling on people that she had been nursing in the past, and who had died, that she took interest in what he was saying. She said to herself, 'My God! He is seeing people from the other side.' When she was going off duty she told the night nurse, 'Keep a close watch on him.' It wasn't that he was in great danger but he was seeing these people.

She also said to a priest, who had come in to anoint someone else, to anoint this man as well. Apparently he continued to see people through the rest of the evening. He died around midnight. When she told me this story she was crying. It was so upsetting for her what she had witnessed.

That same friend also told me that another man became very unwell when she was on duty one day. He had got a heart attack. The ward sister had gone off to her break. They went in and revived the man. When he came around the first thing he said was, 'Where was I? I was just talking to Anne.' What he said didn't mean anything to anybody.

Eventually the ward sister returned from her break and was asking, 'Did anything happen when I was away?' My friend told her, 'This man collapsed and we had to revive him and he came back. But when he came back he said he saw "Anne."' The ward sister knew the man and recognised the name and said, 'That was his first wife.' As it happened, his second wife was outside the door at the time!

I would come across a lot of nurses and I would always be interested in this sort of thing. I always ask them, 'In all your years nursing did you come across anything?' If there's a bunch of us around the table I ask, 'Have you any unusual stories?' Most nurses have at least one story to tell. Everyone has one.

Having been in nursing all my life, I realise that we are all here for a purpose and we are only passing through. When your purpose is done in this world, you move on. There are some people in life who think, 'If I only had six houses or cars!' But I don't think it's important to be interested in material things. It is better to be kind and to know that there is something beyond.

I absolutely believe there is something else there. You don't just go into the ground and that's it, end of story. I know there's a lot more to it. There is a soul and spirit and it goes on. I would feel sorry for anyone that would not believe that there is more. There's an awful lot of peace attached to that and there is nothing to worry about.

OUT-OF-BODY TRAVEL

A woman from Munster, who would prefer to remain anonymous, had an out-of-body experience while comatose in hospital during a serious illness. The event occurred more than four decades ago. 'When I was at the lowest ebb of my sickness they sent for my family and told them that they didn't think I'd pull through,' she explains. 'I was out of it, totally unconscious. I was very, very sick.

'When I came to, they asked me if I could remember anything at all. I said, "Yes. I saw myself being given the last rites." But it wasn't me because I was up in the corner of the room looking down. The body below didn't have any bearing on me because I was out of it, looking in.

'I saw everybody around the bed. The nurse was there and a priest and whoever else. I was being anointed at the time. I was watching it happening but I said nothing. It was like being shown something that was going on beneath you but you weren't it – you were alright and looking at it.

'I didn't feel any pain. I didn't feel anything. I can understand that it's very hard for people to believe that you were actually out of your body. But I know it happened and I can still see myself up there, looking down. It was very strange, most unusual, and something you'd never forget.'

That story, in many ways, typifies the classic out-of-body experience. All the basic elements are there. To begin with, the woman left her body and floated away. As is commonly the case, she was taken by surprise as she discovered that she was outside her physical self. From an overhead position, she observed proceedings beneath her.

She watched as she lay on an operating table surrounded by a team of surgeons and medical staff. She might just as easily have been observing herself dying at the scene of an accident or relaxing on her bed while preparing for an afternoon nap. Alternatively, she might have roamed far away from her body to nearby buildings, over rooftops or to faraway exotic lands – and eventually returned unscathed.

Despite the intrusive, radical surgery she was undergoing down below she felt no pain – which is normally the case with an out-of-body experience. She was also unperturbed by the trauma and turmoil she witnessed as the medical team battled to bring her back from the brink of death.

On her return, she had crystal clear recall of the events that took place. She also developed an interest in spiritual issues, with profound implications for her religious beliefs and her faith. What's more, decades later the experience ranks as one of the most memorable and significant of her life.

Put quite simply, an out-of-body experience is defined as 'the sensation of floating outside of one's body' and, in some cases, 'observing the body from a distance away.' In contrast to a near-death experience, there are unlikely to be bright lights, tunnel travel, meetings with family or friends, or encounters with 'superior beings'. While restricted in scope – although additional elements might sometimes be present – the experience nevertheless is momentous and, as we will see, has implications for where we may be heading when we die.

The adventure normally happens spontaneously, mostly at times when people are feeling comfortable, relaxed and at ease. Some might develop into full-blown near-death experiences, with all that they entail. Most, however, eventually just result in a return to the body. The experiences can also be learned or triggered at will through relaxation techniques and visualisation, or induced through the use of drugs, making them different from the near-death experience.

There are further notable differences between the out-of-body and near-death states. For a start, the majority of those who have out-of-body experiences are in good health at the time, with only ten per cent estimated to be threatened with death. This differs widely from near-death experiences, where people are usually under significant stress.

Many out-of-body travellers are also fearful and worried – sometimes terrified – that they won't be able to return to their physical selves. This, again, is unlike the near-death experience, where the vast majority are calm, at peace and happy with the circumstances they find themselves in. It has also been established that the near-death experience is the more powerful, intense and life-changing of the two.

Other less common features may be present – in particular the linking of the floating body to the physical body by what people often refer to as a 'silver cord'. This thin silver cord, it is reported, is similar to an umbilical cord connecting the out-of-body self to the real body below. Studies vary on how many people report this feature, with estimates ranging from none at all up to one in five.

The concept of the silver cord dates back to Biblical times, where it was prominently noted. The Book of Ecclesiastes tells us clearly and unequivocally that once the silver cord is severed 'the spirit returns to God who gave it' – in other words the person will die. People from other cultures speak of it too, including African tribes where people can neither read nor write.

That the out-of-body experience might be real, and not imaginary, has major implications for the concept of life after death. The supposition that the soul can survive separate from the body is essential to the existence of an afterlife. While the body decays and rots, something – be it a soul, spirit, mind, self or consciousness – must live on.

If the inner self, or mind, can leave the body, as apparently happens with an out-of-body journey, then it follows that the demise of the body doesn't necessarily bring with it the final and ultimate cessation of the self. These, however, are issues which will be touched on in the final chapter. In the meantime, the following are accounts of Irish people who travelled outside of their bodies.

GEMMA, FROM COUNTY MEATH, had a dramatic out-of-body experience after a routine hospital procedure went wrong.

In 1976 I had a myelogram, where they inject dye into the spine to show up an injury. The dye highlights where there might be irregularities. I had a dreadful reaction to it, so they decided they'd remove the dye they put in. It was considered to be a small procedure, involving a light general anaesthetic. It was to take a couple of minutes and then I'd recover and go home.

I was taken off to theatre. After the procedure was over I was brought back to my room and observed for a while. Eventually they thought I was stable enough to leave alone. Everyone thought I was fine, so off they went about their business.

I suddenly began to wheeze badly and have difficulty breathing. I was making dreadful noises in my throat. It was like I was choking, like some sort of spasm. It was like as if my throat had swelled. I was battling for breath and no one was there.

The next thing I was looking down on myself. I was above myself, slightly over to the right, watching. The room was relatively high. It was an extraordinary sensation being up above, up that high. I was looking and I could hear the noise that my throat was making. I was listening and I could hear the dreadful gasping. I was thinking, 'Gosh! I'm not breathing very well. I'd better go and get help. I must find somebody.'

The next thing I recall was being out in the corridor, above everybody, looking down. I was drifting along, very high up because the corridor was higher than the room. At the nurses' station I could see the sister. Sister Hickey was her name. She was in her 40s. She was sitting there, dressed in her navy blue uniform, with her nurse's hat on. She was writing notes and turning around and giving instructions to other people.

I was desperately trying to attract her attention and saying, 'Go back down to the room! I'm in trouble!' No way would she look up and see me. I remember saying, 'Come down quickly! Get up and come down!' I was getting agitated. She wasn't paying any attention because, although there was a part of me there, she couldn't see me. I was not human. But I kept hovering above her while saying, 'Go back down there and sort things out! I can't breathe! Find somebody quickly and help me!'

Suddenly she put her pen down and got up from her desk and drifted down the corridor. I was about three rooms down from her desk. She met a nursing aide on her way and chatted to her for a minute. I was still above her. I was saying, 'Go! Go! Go! Do something quickly! Hurry up! Hurry up! Go in!'

She went in, heard the commotion and saw me struggling to breathe. She hit a buzzer or a bell outside the door and people started running from everywhere. She rushed back in. A couple of doctors came as well. They started pressing on my chest. I was watching and I could hear what they were saying. They were talking about maybe getting somebody else in. Then they put an oxygen mask over my face and I was breathing with this. They also brought a trolley in. They were injecting things into my arms.

All the time I was above them by about two or three feet and I was observing all this. I kept thinking, 'Hurry up! Hurry up!' I was slightly over towards a cupboard, which was along the left as you walked in the door, although at one stage I was behind people and couldn't see over them. I couldn't feel anything. I wasn't taking part in things. I was just watching and leaving it to them.

I could see myself lying on the bed in my pink nightdress. At first I had my hands around my throat as if I was trying to pull something away, but then I was deadly quiet and deadly pale on the bed. I had washed my hair earlier and it looked wet and I was thinking, 'Why isn't it dry?'

I could see them running around saying, 'Get this! Get that! Call such a person!' and so on. I was trying to urge them on, hurry them up. I could see this doctor with a beard and he was running something down my throat. There was somebody else on the other side of the bed. I could see them clearly. I suppose the whole thing took about ten minutes from start to finish.

The next thing I was lying back down on the bed again. I then began to recover and I remember being really breathless and having frightful pressure on my chest. Eventually whatever it was that had happened started to clear. I was left on a drip and began to recover. They observed me a bit more closely and I spent three or four days in hospital.

I recall saying to the sister afterwards, 'I saw what went on in the room.' I said I remembered her telling someone to run for this doctor, the guy with the beard. I said, 'I heard you say to get this and that.' She dismissed it. She thought I was daft. She said, 'You were just dreaming. You were just hallucinating.' But I wasn't hallucinating. I could see everything that was going on. The only one who really listened and took note was an American nurse called Tessa, who was there. She was awestruck when I told her.

Looking back, it was a weird experience and it was very strange to be watching myself down below. I feel maybe I might just have 'gone'. Something did leave my body. I had gone somewhere and I had the ability to observe everything that was going on. I think it made me realise that you can be transported out of your body, and it left me with the knowledge that there has to be another dimension to our lives.

It certainly wasn't a dream. I can still see everybody coming. I can still recall the sensation of suffocating and gasping for air. But I know at the time there was absolutely no spiritual dimension to what happened, from a 'God' point of view. After it, however, I think my belief system was re-created. I had this incredible urge to find some peace again in my faith. And, oftentimes, when I hear about people having an out-of-body experience, I say, 'That happened to me.'

BERNARD, FROM COUNTY MAYO, had his experience in the immediate aftermath of a car crash.

I was alone and on my way home from work one night. It was a beautiful, fine, sunny summer's evening, around 6.30. I was coming up a little slip-road, within a mile of my home. There was a very sharp bend in it, over a river, which I knew very well. As I approached it, I saw this elderly man on a bicycle. He was on the opposite side of the road to me. I just went around the corner, bearing left, presuming everything was fine.

The next thing wasn't there a car coming, overtaking the man on the corner. Apparently the man driving the car, when he saw the cyclist, increased his speed because he thought he would get to the corner before the cyclist did. He was in my path. There was this almighty bang. I will never forget it. The bonnet of my car opened up from the windscreen out. It flicked open and came up over the roof. All I could see was 'Death!', 'Death!', 'Death!' It was written in black letters, coming up in front of my eyes.

The man on the bike knew me and he came knocking on the window. I remember him asking, 'Are you alright? Are you alright?' With the impact of the crash, the dash had come back and hit my right leg at my knee and smashed it. I had a lot of broken ribs as well. I could also hear crying in the other car although I couldn't see the people. It turned out that there was a husband and wife and one child in the car.

Suddenly I was up above, looking down on the crash scene. I was horizontal and floating. I wasn't up that high, probably about 20 feet or so. I could see the two cars entangled in one another down below. I could see the river, which was immediately before the turn. It's a boggy type of area and I could see the fields around. The area I could see was like a circle, like what you would see looking through a pipe.

I felt very calm and very peaceful. I wasn't panicking. There was no pain. I couldn't see myself and I couldn't see anyone in the other car, but I could see the man with the bike and the ground around. The man was still at my car. He was still knocking at the window and asking, 'Are you alright? Are you alright?' I thought I was gone.

The view was strange because when you look down on something there's a totally different perspective. I sometimes go to England on holidays and we fly back into Knock Airport. When you are above the ground, and coming in to land, you are trying to recognise different places. The only thing you can easily recognise is the Charlestown to Knock road. You cross over that and the runway is immediately after it. It's very hard to recognise anything else. It's a different perspective altogether. But at the crash scene I could see everything.

This all happened over two or three minutes. I then came back to myself again. I didn't realise the injuries I had. I got out of the car not knowing anything about my knee. I fell on the ground and couldn't move. I could still hear the crying in the other car, although it turned out later that they were fine. I then started saying to the man, 'Watch the traffic! Watch the traffic!' I was afraid another car would come and that would be the end. He did watch the traffic and stopped cars on either side.

I was lying on the ground at the back of my own car when the ambulance arrived. They took me to hospital. I was quite alert. When I got to the hospital I discovered that my knee – I think they call it the patella – was smashed to smithereens. The pain was horrendous. The doctor couldn't do anything with it. He said, 'I can put in a plastic unit but the problem is it will have to be replaced every so often. You will have to go through the same procedure again.' So he then removed it altogether.

For a long time after, any time I travelled in a car I had to sit in the back seat and I had to have my head covered. I couldn't sit in the front. Eventually I got the courage to sit behind the wheel again. It took me about a year to drive once more. When I started driving again, I was OK. Yet every time I drive past that spot – which I do frequently – I always remember what happened. On the anniversary date I always say, 'This is my anniversary. I could be dead so many years now.' I always thank God I'm alive.

MARY KENNY, FROM COUNTY GALWAY, floated away from her body during an unusually traumatic childbirth.

We had twins in November 1992 and they were stillborn. They had actually died in September, at seven months, but I had to carry them nearly to term because I had a medical problem. Eventually they were delivered in the maternity ward in the hospital, at 6.20 in the evening. During the delivery I became very ill. I was losing a lot of blood and there was a lot of panic around.

I was in so much pain and distress. They were trying to get blood into me but it was just running in and out. All my veins had collapsed. I couldn't bear the thought of another needle. I really had enough of it. I couldn't take any more. They kept on saying, 'Stay with us! Stay with us! You have to stay with us! You have to come back!' They were slapping me on the face, trying to get me back.

Suddenly I was just floating over my body. I was up at the ceiling, lying face downwards. I was looking down and I could see myself below. It was all so clear and so real. I looked so white. I had no fear. I saw my husband, Michael, who was sitting beside me rubbing my hand. There was a good friend there also but he was asked to leave. The consultant was there and the anaesthetist. And there were a few nurses too.

I saw the twins over in a corner at the window. The two of them were together in a plastic cot. I had never seen them up to then. I couldn't have seen them from where I was in the bed. They weren't near me at all. They were actually in a little area off at the side of the room. But they were very visible to me from where I was up above.

The twins were dead and there were no clothes on them. It was a November night, with terrible weather. It was belting rain. All the windows were open because the room was so warm. The wind was blowing and the curtain was blowing over them. I suppose they had to keep the windows open because there were so many people in the small space. I thought it was so sad that there was no one to look after the twins.

I also saw all the blood from up above. It was everywhere. I think it was 16 units of blood I got but it kept going in and out. It was flowing on the floor, under the bed. I could see that. They just couldn't stop the bleeding. There was terrible panic. I don't know if they were saying 'She is gone!' but I can definitely remember them saying, 'Come back to me! Come back to me!'

There was another strange aspect to it concerning a man in the hospital mortuary, near to where Maternity was. I knew the man but didn't know he had died. Yet when I was out of my body I was aware he was there. I remember asking my husband, a day or two later, if that particular man had died. He said, 'Yeah. His funeral has already taken place.' So he was in the mortuary at the time although I wouldn't have known he had died. That also happened when I was out of my body.

Eventually they put me on a stretcher, to take me to theatre. I was still up above, looking at what was going on. They went to wheel me out. I was still up there when I came to the door, which was actually below me. But I didn't go out. Instead they stopped. They said, 'She has stopped bleeding.' I didn't have to go to theatre. Suddenly I was back again in my body and I ended up in Intensive Care after that. I had four other children and it was like I was being left to rear them.

In time I went on to have a bigger family but I still feel the twins are close to me and I called them Fiona and Michael. I also wouldn't be afraid to die although I would be sorry for my loved ones. But, looking back even all these years later, what went on that evening in 1992 is still very clear in my mind. I feel I was going somewhere or had gone somewhere. It was just that it wasn't my time.

CHRIS, FROM COUNTY WICKLOW, left her body while critically ill as a young child.

I was only a little child, around four, very small. I was very sick and I must have been unconscious. I was on the way out, I would say, although I didn't know what was wrong with me. I was in the front upstairs bedroom, which was my parents' room. I must have been brought in there because I was so sick. They were very concerned and worried. They wouldn't have made such a fuss if I hadn't been so bad.

The next thing I was gone from the bed and was sitting on the window-ledge. I am 100 per cent sure I had died. I was totally myself, as I am, or as I was then. I was out of my body, over by the window although I could still see my body in the bed.

I could see there were five people around the bed – my mother and father, my grandmother, a nurse and a doctor. I remember looking at them and seeing them. I could hear their voices. I saw from their faces how upset they were. They were extremely worried and concerned. I just sat there, looking around and wondering, 'What is my mother crying for? What are these people upset for?'

Then I remember waking up in the bed and they were still there. I had come back into the bed. I can remember coming to and seeing everyone around me. I eventually got better although I wasn't too well for a while. My mother had a problem with my health. I was very anaemic but she cured it. Yet I never forgot what happened. It has stayed with me all my life, down through the decades.

Later on in life I spoke to a person who had a serious accident. She was on one of those water slides and got a huge kick in the chest. Her heart stopped. She went to the bottom and was under the water for a long time before anyone missed her. There was nobody there to help, absolutely no one. She was unconscious, with her heart stopped. And she did die.

Her husband resuscitated her. He was into first aid and things like that. He did what he could and then the ambulance came and took her away. When they got her to the hospital, they told them that her heart had stopped and she had died. She had gone into a new life for a while.

She told me a wonderful story about what happened. She said that her whole life had flashed before her eyes. She saw it all, her whole life. She felt it was the Lord showing her what her life was like. It was a happy experience. So these things can happen. I have no doubt about it.

Looking back on my own experience, I am sure I had died. I think I must have passed away, that my heart had stopped. It would have to have stopped for me to die and for my spirit to depart. I believe it was my inner being that had left my body. It was the part inside of me that God created for himself.

The experience has probably brought me closer to God. I have a firm belief in God to this day. I now believe that when you die, it's like you are shedding an old coat. You end up the way you are, with the same hair, eyes, hands and feet and everything. It's your whole body, as it is. You are not a ghost or anything. You are not even aware you are dead.

What happened was amazing and has stayed with me all my life. I never forgot it all down through the decades. I don't really know what happened. I was just in bed one minute and the next minute out of the bed. I get great joy out of the story now. I'm very happy about it and I'm not afraid of death because of my relationship with God. If he wants me today, I'm ready to go.

TRUDY WATSON had an out-of-body experience back in 1950. It happened shortly after she contracted polio. Trudy was living in Carrickfergus, County Antrim, at the time.

I was 25 years old and just home from a holiday in the Isle of Man. I had gone there with my husband and my little boy, who was two-and-a-half. My boy was playing in the garden. He was playing with his hands out, pretending to be a Spitfire. He tripped and fell. You should have seen his nose. He had a bright red plum of blood for a nose. He had bruises. His face had flattened completely. He was in quite a lot of pain.

I brought him down the hill to the doctor's place. The doctor reassured me that no bones were broken and so on. He told me to use a cold compress, the usual. We walked back up the hill and I put David to bed. I then sat down. It was a hot July day and I had been sweating coming up the hill, so I sat by an open window. Later on I went to bed.

David woke me up, crying. He was saying, 'Mummy! Mummy!' I went in to see him and I realised I couldn't bend my neck. I had to move my shoulders, neck and head all together. I thought I had a chill after sitting with a sweaty neck and with cold air coming in on it. I went back to bed thinking nothing of it.

The next morning, when I woke up, I was trying to make sandwiches for my husband to take to work and I was having difficulty making out how to cut the bread. My husband said to me, 'Are you OK?' I said, 'No. I feel funny.' My husband said, 'I'll get the doctor.' Down came the doctor and he said, 'I can feel paralysis starting.' I said, 'I hope it isn't infantile paralysis.' That is what polio was called in those days – it was mostly in children.

He said I had better go down to the local hospital to see what was wrong. Off I went, being sick all the way down. Initially, in the hospital, I could sit up. Then I couldn't sit up. I felt all wobbly, with no power. Then one leg wouldn't move over. Then another one wouldn't move back. I was gradually becoming paralysed.

I got a lumbar puncture there, which is awful. It was agonising. I can still feel it. They did it twice. Eventually they got a brain specialist down from the Royal Victoria Hospital in Belfast. He drew off fluid from my brain and he was very good.

The next day I couldn't move at all. I couldn't move anything. I was completely and utterly paralysed inside and out. I could not even spend a penny. They had to feed me. They sent me to Purdysburn Fever Hospital in Belfast. Up I went. I was put into a side ward on my own because I was the only adult.

The doctor came around. I remember I could read things upside down and I could follow what he was writing even though it was upside down. I saw that he had written 'acute anterior poliomyelitis.' I had polio!

I woke up during the middle of that same night, about three o'clock in the morning, and the first thing I thought was, 'Thank God! All the pain is gone. Isn't it great?' It was dark but not pitch-black. It was such a beautiful feeling. All my nerves had been on fire up to that. But there was no pain. It was glorious. I couldn't believe it. I wondered could I sit up. And I could. I sat up in slow motion. But the biggest joy was that there was no pain.

As I sat up, I realised I was not in my bed but on a black wooden plinth. This wooden plinth was about three or four feet off the ground, with me on top of it. It was like a cata-falque, which a queen's or king's coffin would be laid out on top of. You would see it in Westminster Abbey, with the coffin lying on top. It was a solid thing, made of wood. It was like ebony wood and quite comfortable. The wood was warm and it was moving very slowly, centimetre by centimetre, towards the door of the side ward.

I lay down again on the plinth. Then I decided to sit up again. It was such a joy to be able to do it. It was great to be able to move after so long not being able to move an eyelash. So I sat up again and I looked to my left. There was a white wall, with white tiles, as you would get in a fever hospital.

I then looked in front and there was the door. I was going slowly towards it. Everything, including me, seemed to be moving towards the door. Then I looked to the right and there was another white-tiled wall except there was a bed there too, about three feet away – and in the bed was me!

The view that I saw was of me lying down in my ordinary hospital bed, well tucked in. The face that I saw was flushed with a high temperature. It was shiny. I was clear as a bell. I thought, 'That's me!' I just accepted that it was me in the bed. But the real me was on the plinth – that was Trudy Watson. It shows that you can disengage yourself quite quickly.

I looked back again at the door. I knew that I would turn right outside the door and go up an ordinary corridor. There was no bright light or no people waiting for me or anything, just that I would go up this corridor. I think I was heading into the beyond. It was so strange. I just accepted what was happening. And I was so grateful that I had no pain and I was very happy.

Suddenly I heard a child calling out, 'Mummy! Mummy! Mummy!' I thought, 'That's David.' It was a child of about two-and-a-half, the same age. I found myself scrabbling out of that wooden bed to get to the door, to see my son that I hadn't seen for three days. Instead I found myself back in the real bed and the black plinth had disappeared. I never made it out the door on the plinth. I was on my way but the child brought me back.

I was eight or nine months in hospital. I could only walk about five steps before I got out. But, once I got out, I went back to living a normal life. I later met the consultant who had looked after me. This was 30 or 40 years later. I had an appointment with him on a separate issue but I brought in photographs to remind him of who I really was. I said, 'There's me and that's my wee son David.' He said, 'But Mrs. Watson, you don't need to show me that. We all remember you.' I said, 'How do you mean?' And he said, 'We thought you were going to die – but you didn't.'

I then told him about my out-of-body experience and I asked him, 'Do you think that was the moment of death?' He said, 'Definitely!' He also said, 'I'm sure, if I looked, that would be the date we thought you would probably die. That was the point of death. But the next day you were still there. And we were surprised.'

I also always wondered who that little child was who called, 'Mummy! Mummy! Mummy!' I didn't say anything to anybody for years because I thought people would say, 'That woman is odd.' Eventually, however, I was asked to talk before the Northern Ireland Polio Fellowship at their annual dinner. The first thing I asked those who were there was if anybody had been in Purdysburn Fever Hospital around 23 July 1950.

Three people put their hands up. Two were there on the wrong dates. But one woman was the right age – about a year and ten months – and was there at that date. I said, 'I think I have found you. You brought me back to life. I was dying.

You cried and, as a result, I came back.' It was she saved my life. It was all thanks to her.

JOAN, WHO ORIGINALLY COMES FROM DUBLIN but who lives in Kent, England, travelled away from her body during a beating from her mother. Although the incident happened way back in 1948, she remembers it clearly to this day.

I was just eight years old at the time and we lived with my grandparents in Dublin. My dad had left us when we were kids. He left us a matter of months after my little brother died. We went straight to my grandparents. My mum wasn't doing too well. She was losing her temper with me a lot. She was hitting me about. She didn't seem to be able to stop. Somebody else always had to stop her. She just couldn't cope.

My cousins also lived with my grandparents and one day one of them had a birthday. He was three months older than me and we were close. It must have been August time because his birthday is 31 August. He hadn't received a birthday card yet from his mum, who lived in England. He was upset. So I took some pennies that the gasman had left and bought him a present. I got a beating from my mum, as a result, because I had done something wrong.

My mum started beating me downstairs and she then dragged me upstairs. The bedroom was shut and she was knocking me about. It was a terrible beating. It was life-threatening because it gave me a collapsed lung. Suddenly I switched off to what was happening to me. I stopped thinking about me.

I didn't feel that I was being badly beaten. I didn't have any conscious notion of the bedroom at all. Instead I was suddenly looking at my grandmother, who was an invalid, from up on a height. She was trying to get up the stairs to stop my mum from hitting me. She was trying to rescue me.

What I remember happening – and I have never forgotten it – was that I was looking down at her as she was climbing the stairs. I was above her head. I must have been around ceiling height, stuck to the ceiling or something. Physically I was back in the bedroom but otherwise I was up at the ceiling above the stairs. I can remember she had a long skirt on, which was what she normally wore. She had a coloured crochet shoulder thing around her.

She was looking up to the top of the stairs and saying, 'Please stop! Please stop! Someone stop her! Oh, my God! She will kill her!' She was holding onto the wall, on each side, and she was really struggling. There was a wall, and not a rail, at both sides of the stairs and she had a hand on each of the walls.

She was slowly lifting her feet to try to come up. But I knew she couldn't do it. She hadn't been able to climb the stairs for 16 years previous to that. I was very panicky that she would fall. I was worried something would happen to her.

My cousin was trying to get up behind her but my grandmother was blocking him from getting past. She was a big woman and was blocking the stairs. He was also trying to come up to stop my mum from hitting me. All this time I was shouting to my grandmother, 'Please don't climb the stairs!'

I don't know if she heard me or not. And I don't think she even saw me but I can't understand why. What I do know, however, is that she never made it up to the top. I think she only came up about three steps, although I think my cousin did make it up. This all probably went on for five minutes or so.

I don't remember how the beating came to a stop and I don't remember coming back to my body. I don't even remember seeing the room again until I woke up the next day. I was bruised and hurt and I couldn't go to school. When I did go to school, a couple of days later, the nun thought I was quite ill and asked my mum to take me to the doctor. The nun was right because I had a collapsed lung.

The beating resulted in my being admitted to the hospital. From there I was put into a children's home. For two-and-a-half years I was in and out of this home. But I eventually learned to forgive my mum. She was having difficulties and she had a lot going on for her at the time. I really looked after her when she was in her old age. I also think back on what happened a lot. It was all so real. It's never left my memory.

I know it happened although I cannot tell you how it did. It's always been such a mystery to me. Everybody in the family knows about it because I told them. It's still talked about. But I don't know how it was possible for me to have seen her in that situation. Later on, when I heard of out-of-body experiences, I wondered, 'Could that have been what happened to me?' Perhaps it was, although I still don't understand it to this day.

KRISTIAN SHORTT, FROM COUNTY DONEGAL, who was the victim of a near-fatal stabbing in 2008, went on an out-of-body journey and experienced a visit from his dead brother.

I was stabbed thirteen times – four times in the neck, three in the chest, three in the head, two in my hand and one in my back. It happened over a silly, drunken argument. The guy lifted a knife and started sticking me with it.

My jugular and my carotid artery in my neck were slashed open. I had two punctured lungs. I was stabbed into the throat and my vocal cords were slashed. I got my head fractured in two places with the stabbings to my head. I was stabbed into my stomach. The medical records are a book thick.

I tried to stay on my feet to fend him off but I was losing my energy and my air because my lungs were punctured. I began to fall and he kept stabbing me while I was falling. I found myself lying in a big pool of blood and losing consciousness. I was just draining away.

I blacked out. The feeling was kind of gradual but quick at the same time. I knew that I was about to die. I didn't get any visions or anything at that time. I didn't even know there was an ambulance coming. The ambulance came because another guy had called it. I only had about a pint-and-a-half of blood left by the time the ambulance arrived.

I was taken to the hospital, where I had two life-saving operations. I have a memory, when I was out cold in hospital, of being at the edge of a cliff, kind of hovering over the edge of it. I don't know what I was dressed in because I didn't look down at myself. It was night-time and it was dark. It was a windy night.

I felt a warm breeze blowing through me. The breeze was all around me. Like if you go to a cliff tonight you're going to get breeze – it was the exact same thing except it was warm. It was a lovely feeling. It seemed like it was Ireland but I wasn't cold at all like it would have been on an Irish cliff.

There was water maybe 50 metres down. I could hear the waves but I couldn't see them. The cliff went vertically down and the waves were crashing up against the bottom. I was on the edge. I was kind of standing vertically but I was leaning backwards at about 45 degrees. I was mainly staring at the sky. The sky was clear, the stars were out, and it was full of stars.

I was hovering higher and higher, with every second, into space. I started to hover up towards the sky. I felt a kind of weightlessness, like I was magic. I didn't have any thoughts. It was just nothingness, nothing going through my head. I felt myself being elevated up towards the sky.

I hovered up about ten feet and then, suddenly, I felt myself coming back down again. For some reason, I started coming back towards the ground. It ended with me waking up about five or six hours later in Intensive Care.

Later on I was told I had died during my second operation, on the operating table. I had died for 10 or 15 seconds or so and they had to use the defibrillator to get me back. That happened within the first couple of days. The time when I was coming back to the ground must have been when I was being saved. I wasn't able to ask my family about it or communicate with anybody. In fact, I wasn't able to speak until about two weeks after I was stabbed. But it was more than likely that time, about two days after the stabbing.

I also saw a vision of my brother, who had died 35 years before. I was lying in my bed in Intensive Care. He was looking at me and smiling. He didn't say anything. He did nothing, just smiled. He was sitting there, looking. It was just his figure and there was kind of a haze around him. It was a whitey-blue haze. My brother was about three or four years old when he died. I had never met him before because he died before I was born. But, when he appeared to me, he was the same age he was when he died.

I have looked back at photos of him and I saw him as he was. He looked the exact same way as he did in the pictures, except that he was sitting like a Buddha, the way they sit with their legs crossed. He was naked. He was baby skinned, with a whitey-tanned skin on him. He had long blond hair, like he had in real life. It didn't last very long, about five or ten seconds.

I was conscious, as far as I know, for that. Again I think it was about two or three days after the stabbing, although I don't know if it was before or after my other experience. I can't place the time. At that stage I still only had about a 20 or 30 per cent chance of surviving. I was in great danger for about four or five days. I was also still in shock from the whole thing that was going on and I was still trying to come to grips with the trauma that had just happened to me.

Initially I thought my brother had come to get me. I thought he had come to take me away. But it was obviously for something else. I think he was looking after me, watching out for me. It was certainly a surreal experience. My family are completely mystified by it. It has definitely reinforced their beliefs. But they are happy to know there is something there. I also feel that when I die I will meet my brother again.

Before this I was afraid of death, but I have no fear of dying anymore. Not one bit. I died already, a very horrific death. I was stabbed to death, so I got one of the worst deaths that you can imagine. No other death can compare to that again. Most people say that I'm a 'dead man walking.' So I don't have any fear. And I also definitely feel there's somewhere nice to go to when we die.

DAVID GASCOYNE, WHO LIVES IN COUNTY LIMERICK, had a heart attack and an out-of-body experience during a holiday in Barbados. David, who was aged 42 at the time, was accompanied by his wife Maria.

In 1996 I went on holiday with my wife to Barbados. It was a two-week holiday. At the end of the first week I got up in the morning and got a bit of a pain in my chest. It was a niggling pain in the centre of my chest. I took no notice. I went into the living-room of the apartment and opened up the patio door. I made a cup of tea and lit up a cigarette. I still had the pain but I thought it was a bit of indigestion. It was a continual, stabbing pain, like a bit of a pin sticking in you.

I told my wife. She said, 'Take a couple of Rennies.' I made a cup of tea and a bit of toast. I lay down for a bit because the pain was getting more persistent. It was also getting sharper. Then I got up and went into the living area and I sat there by the wooden coffee-table, which was about 2' 6" high. There was nothing on the table and it had chairs around it. I was stripped to the waist and dressed in my shorts. Maria was in the bedroom. It was roughly around nine o'clock in the morning.

The next thing – bang! I had gone out cold. I had fallen over from the seat onto the top of the table, head first. The lights had gone out, there was nobody at home! All Maria heard was the air coming out of my mouth and a bang or a thump on the table as my head hit off it. Maria came running through from the bedroom. I was lying over the table. My arms were stretched out over it.

The next thing I can remember is a floating sensation. I was up about ceiling height, about eight feet high, and I was looking right down onto the crown of my head and across my shoulders. I was hovering up above. I could see down on top of me. I was looking through my eyes at me down below and spread-eagled across the table. I could see the top of my head and my arms stuck out wide beside me. It was like an aerial shot of me lying across the table.

The real me was looking down on the other me. I was away from my body and detached from it. The real me was up above and what was down below was just what was left. Everything was light, not dark. I wasn't looking down a tunnel or anything like that. It was very quiet. I was very calm. It was as if I was saying, 'What has happened?' I couldn't grasp what was going on.

Then I heard a voice saying, 'Dave, what are you doing up here?' That was the weirdest thing. It wasn't a voice that I had heard before. It wasn't my dad's voice or anything like that. It was definitely a male voice but it was youngish and very ordinary. Then the door banged and I sort of took a deep breath. The impact of the door made me jump. The next thing I was back down again.

Apparently Maria had gone running downstairs and out the door to get some help. She had left the front door open. What we think happened was that the wind blew through the apartment and slammed the door shut with a big, mighty bang. That bang, it seems, made me jump and forced me to take a breath. I sat up from the table into the chair. I was sort of jolted into coming around. That's probably what brought me back.

I could hear voices outside the door, which was now locked. It was Maria with a couple of people from the hotel, including paramedics. They were discussing whether to kick the door in. They got the shock of their lives because I opened the door to them. I said, 'What are you doing out there?'

They were talking then about how to get me down the stairs. They were going to put me in a chair and carry me down. I said, 'No. You will probably drop me.' So I walked down and got into the back of this little ambulance and they drove me to the hospital.

I had an X-Ray. A fellow came in to me and said, 'You have had a heart attack. Your lips have gone blue.' I wouldn't accept it and I still felt calm. He said, 'You've had a big heart attack, believe me.' He said, 'I know you smoke. I can smell it on your breath. So don't tell me you don't smoke.' It went from there and I was in Intensive Care for a week. I then had to stop there for another three weeks before they would let me come back home.

I was lucky. They said the arteries on the left side had become a bit clogged. The cardiologist, who was brilliant, said, 'Normally when somebody has a heart attack it leaves a bit of a scar across the heart, like a watermark. But you haven't got one. You've had a big heart attack yet you've got away with it scot-free.' But when I came home I had to change my ways, especially regarding dieting and smoking and watching what I was doing.

I look back on it as a very narrow escape and a wake-up call. I have been OK ever since. Since then dying has never really bothered me. The only thing that bothers me is the way I die. I wouldn't want to die in a fire or drown or anything like that. I would love to go in my sleep, from old age. But death doesn't worry me.

I remember telling the cardiologist in Barbados about looking down on top of myself. He said, 'I've heard that before, with different patients.' He was coy about it. But I definitely think I was leaving my body and heading off to somewhere else. And I do think there is something there afterwards. At least I was going up! But, as for Barbados, I've only been there that one time and I'd like to think I'll see it the next time I go back.

PETER O'KELLY, FROM COUNTY WICKLOW, had a strange experience while on a visit to Japan.

In June 1991 I was offered a tour of Japan. I went with a business friend of mine. It was a fantastic offer. It was ten days in all, to Tokyo, Fuji, Hakone, Osaka, Kyoto and places like that. One day we left the hotel in Tokyo, at about half past nine in the morning, to go to Mount Fuji. As you can imagine from the fact that it was morning, alcohol doesn't enter into this story. Nor did I have a hangover, as I had no drink the night before. I wasn't feeling sick either and wasn't suffering from food poisoning. I was perfectly healthy, feeling wonderful.

I was relaxing and joking while we were waiting for the coach. We struck up a relationship with this English couple. We got onto the coach and we headed out into open countryside. We left the suburbs of Tokyo and were heading to Mount Fuji. There was this Japanese guy who was cracking jokes in English and everybody was laughing. There was great hilarity and I was laughing away.

All of a sudden, for no reason, I felt as if I wanted to vomit. I felt absolutely horrendous. After a short while I asked for the coach to be stopped. I got off but I couldn't throw anything up. I ran my fingers down my throat. Nothing happened. I literally staggered back onto the coach and sat down. I felt I was going mad. I felt that I wasn't myself, sitting there.

I felt that I was outside my body, looking at myself. It was an extraordinary feeling, which is hard to describe. I saw myself sitting there and knew I was on a coach. I knew my friend was beside me but I felt absolutely, totally weird. I felt I had died and was looking at myself from a few feet away.

I wondered, 'What's this?' I said to my friend, 'You have got to look after me because I am just after going mad. I'm not responsible for any actions of mine.' It was crazy. I just wanted the Japanese guy to shut up or I would strangle him.

Eventually, after an hour or an hour-and-a-half, we arrived at our destination and we all had to get off the coach. I was still feeling awful. As I got off the bus, the Englishman we had made friends with in Tokyo said, 'My God! What's wrong with you? Your face is after collapsing. You are grey. What is gone wrong?' I said, 'I just don't know, it's weird.'

Everyone else went into the interpretative centre while I

just wandered off over to a sort of a cliff. I felt I wanted to throw myself off it. I sat on the edge of the cliff and I remember distinctly there were ponies down below and I could smell the dung.

I eventually got up and staggered back to the bus. People said, 'Take your time. We won't let the bus leave without you.' I got onto it and I flopped down on the seat. The bus headed off to our next destination, which was lunch in a hotel. I was still like a zombie and felt absolutely brutal.

As we headed down, the bus was quiet. The engine was very subdued and all I can remember hearing was the swish of the tyres. Even the Japanese guide, who earlier was going on and cracking jokes, had gone quiet. I went to sleep and woke up probably ten minutes later.

I felt not 100 per cent but OK after I woke up. I went in and ate a five-course lunch. I even forgot all about the incident. We then went across a nearby lake in a sailing-ship, taking photographs and laughing and joking. We went in a cable-car, everything that you do as a tourist.

We then drove down to our hotel in a place called Hakone and started to prepare for a night's entertainment. I was in great form. We were laughing and joking about the night ahead, which was a geisha night, wondering if there would be geisha girls there and all that.

In the hotel I popped my head out through the window of my room. As I did so, this Englishman I had been talking to earlier put his head out through his window. He looked at me and said, 'God! You are grand now. You were grand this morning. But whatever happened, you looked terrible, just like death, up Mount Fuji.' I said, 'I know. You're just after reminding me of it.' He said, 'It was pretty weird.' He also said to me, 'Are you psychic, by any chance?' I said, 'Certainly not, far from it, the last person in the world.'

As I was talking to him, the phone rang. I said to him, 'Excuse me.' I went over to it, thinking it was reception. I picked it up and it was one of my sons saying that my other son's daughter had been killed. He said, 'Gráinne is dead.' I said, 'What?' I wondered what he was talking about. I couldn't take it in. She would have been four in a month. I was thinking, 'I'm in Japan. What are you ringing me with stupid talk like that for?'

It didn't sink in. He said, 'Dad, she is dead.' I thought she had got meningitis or something. He said, 'She was hit by a car crossing the road and killed instantly.' As it transpired, she was crossing the road to show her new dress to her dad and a car hit her. She was well across the road when she was hit. That's what happened.

It turned out that she was killed roughly around the same time I felt sick and was looking at myself from outside my body. I figure she came looking for me. We were exactly alike. There was a picture of me in the pram as a kid. Everyone thought it was her. Even she thought it was her. We were very close. We were of a like mind and I think she came looking for me.

I have often wondered about it. I'm not a very religious kind of guy. I was brought up to be religious by a mother who made me go to rosary and benediction and all this stuff. But I have grave doubts about it and I don't believe in a man with a long beard, sitting on a cloud, with the Son and the Holy Ghost.

Years later I told the story to a friend of mine and she said, 'Maybe you had a minor heart attack.' Well, if I did I got rid of it very easily and it was a very quick heart attack. It also can't be just a coincidence – that would be stretching it. It was just too much. That it happened around the same time certainly shook me quite a bit. It was a weird experience and

I often wonder about it. I remember it in exact detail to this day.

SINGER MICKEY HARTE, FROM COUNTY DONEGAL, tells how as a child he floated above his body after falling into a stream and hitting his head.

I was about three years old and I was down in a place called Ardbane, which is my mum's ancestral home. It is close to Downings in County Donegal, right on the north-west coast. We used to go down there all the time and visit. It's a beautiful place. It was probably a Sunday visit, just a day-trip.

We were out playing around the garden and the yard. It's a fairly enclosed place, right at the bottom of a road and there's no other traffic on it. It's just a laneway down to this house, so it's safe and secluded for kids. But, suddenly, somebody noticed I had gone missing.

I had fallen into a little river, which we would call a burn. I had rambled to it. It was just in front of the house, down at the end of the street. It's like a trickle of water in the summertime, although in really heavy weather it fills up more. It would need to be raining for weeks before there would be any kind of a run in it at all. I must have stumbled in there and went over. There were rocks in it and I just banged my head. I can't remember much after that, although I would have been lying on top of the rocks.

I remember, however, that I had an out-of-body experience. I remember seeing myself lying down below in the burn. I could see myself from up above. I was just hovering there, watching myself. I wasn't miles up in the sky. I was fairly close, about 20 feet up, about roof height.

I saw myself below, lying in a foetal position, as if I was in the womb. I think I had a jumper and short trousers on. I wasn't moving. I was completely still, lying on my right-hand side. I could see myself there. I was comfortable. It wasn't turbulent. It was all peaceful surroundings. I was just staring down, looking at this picture. But, down below, I can't remember myself lying there at all.

It was a completely clear picture of myself. It was very strong and very vivid. That part of it is strange because you'd wonder how as a child you could see yourself down there in that position. You'd wonder how you could even think of that as a kid, how you could conceptualise it. But it was exactly as I was. I don't remember how long it lasted. I'd say it lasted a few minutes. And I didn't feel upset about it at all.

My brother and sister eventually came looking for me and they found me. I have a vague recollection of them wakening me up. I had been knocked unconscious. I also have some recollection of them getting me out of the burn. They brought me up to the house and my mum says she brought me to the doctor up in Carrigart. He checked it out and said it was OK. She thinks I got stitches somewhere in my head.

I told my mum about it instantly and sometimes we talked about it later on. She'd ask me about it. But I don't know what it was. I didn't have any lights pulling me or anything like that. You'd hear about stories like that. You'd also hear people saying that when somebody has lost someone he might have been dead for a few minutes, they might have to resuscitate him, and people would have experiences then. It's often crossed my mind that that could be the case with me. If it was, then it wasn't my time.

It's still a very clear memory to me after all these years. I can still see it and occasionally it will come back to me. I still go to where it happened a lot. I feel really at home there. The spot where it happened hasn't changed at all. But it mystifies me to this day what it was.

For me it was a pleasant experience. It's not something I look back on and go, 'God! I never want to go through that again.' There was something empowering about it. It didn't feel that I was out of control. But it was very weird and I've never experienced anything like it since.

LAURALEAF, WHO COMES FROM COUNTY WATERFORD but who now lives in County Wicklow, found she could leave her body at will following a near-drowning back in the early 1970s.

When I was eight I was down on the rocks in Dunmore East, where I lived. I was with my two sisters, who were aged 10 and 11. I had begged them to bring me with them. We used to run and dodge the waves where the foam would come up. But this day there was a storm and when I was down there with them I got hit by lightning on the leg and I was dragged into the sea by a wave.

I remember being pulled in by this mass of water. I could see grey and silver, which is what the sea is like when your eyes are open. I didn't know what was happening. I don't remember anything after that but my 11-year-old sister jumped in and saved me. She dragged me out onto a rock and gave me the kiss of life. Eventually my sisters got me home and I was out for the count and confined to bed.

One day, while lying in bed, I was thinking, 'Oh, God! I can't get to sleep.' Suddenly I started feeling that my body was five times bigger than it was. I felt myself bursting out of it. I felt myself losing the life in my body. I ended up floating and looking at myself down on the bed. I was a good height up, right at the top of the ceiling, where you couldn't go any further. I could see myself in the bed below, asleep with my 'Leo the Lion' toy.

I must have done it 12 or 13 times over about a year. I could make it happen. I used to try it out to entertain myself. I'd say, 'I'll do it one more time.' I thought it was cool. I felt really powerful. I was always awake when I did it. And I always felt myself to be the person up above looking down. I was never the person lying on the bed looking up. I thought it was amazing looking down on myself.

The last one I had was very scary because I felt I couldn't get back down again. I was up there and my eyes were closed. I felt they were locked. I had been looking down at myself but suddenly I couldn't see myself below. I was trying to force my eyes open. I was really afraid because I couldn't open them or move a muscle. I thought I was dying. Eventually I did make it back although I decided not to mess around with it again. So I stopped making it happen after that. I would do something else like read and read until I fell asleep.

Looking back, I'm convinced that I left my body. The experiences were all definitely real to me. And it was strange how they affected me. When I would draw myself in school I would always draw myself from above, looking down. Yet I never said it to anyone else. I suppose I thought it was something that everyone did. But while I thought it was normal, I always thought it was not normal as well. It was always a bit of a mystery to me.

ROBERT ALEXANDER JONES tells how his father, Robert James Jones, travelled out of his body while being revived after a heart attack. They lived at the time in Bangor, County Down.

My dad was in the British Army for 28 years and was a real hero during the Second World War. He came through some horrendous battles. He actually was a mascot for the Durham and Somerset Light Infantry. The magazine for the Light Infantry was called *Light Bob* and my dad was on the front of it.

He always said he joined the army to get a pair of boots. Our family came from Armagh, where they all ran about barefoot. There was a lot of poverty. He and his best friend used to caddy and they did it in their bare feet. So they joined the army to get the boots. He ended up fighting the Japanese and the Germans. He was in the desert too, in Egypt.

He told me that one day he and this other fellow were stuck in the middle of a big German barrage and a British barrage. They were near a church. The guy that was with him jumped out of the hole they were in and started running towards the church. He was hit by a shell and killed. So my dad faced death a lot in his life.

Unfortunately he always smoked heavily. He told me he smoked 200 Woodbines that time during the barrage. They used to come in tins. They were very strong. As a result, he developed heart troubles when he was in his early 40s while still in the army. The doctors told him he had to stop smoking cigarettes so he took up the pipe instead.

Eventually, in the early 1980s, he developed serious heart problems. His health was deteriorating. He was always bordering on taking these heart attacks. The doctors said his valves were closing themselves off. When they eventually took him into the hospital they said, 'We want to do a bypass.' He said, 'What are my chances?' They said, '50-50.' He said, 'I'm not prepared to take that chance.'

In time he was taken into a local hospital with chest pains. The tradition then was to hand out Guinness to everybody in the hospital. They thought it was good for them. My dad didn't feel quite so bad so he would go around to people who were really ill and ask them if they wanted their Guinness. If they didn't, he took it. Because of that, they presumed that he was fine and ended up releasing him from the hospital that night. But a very short while afterwards he was brought back into hospital as an emergency.

This time he was brought into the Belfast City Hospital. The doctors sent him to Ward 18, which was the main ward. He took a big heart attack. He said, 'It was like someone grabbing your heart and squeezing it.' He went unconscious. They rushed him down a narrow corridor from the main ward. You go into the right, which is a special place where someone who has taken a heart attack is brought into. They have all the defibrillators and stuff in there to start your heart again.

My dad later said that he rose above himself in that room and was looking down on everything that was happening. He said he was floating above his body, looking at himself. He saw himself on what he thought was a table. He had died. He saw three doctors standing around him.

The doctors were working on him to revive him. They put these things on his chest and shocked him. They were the defibrillator pads. He never said how high up he was but if he could see the three guys standing around him he must have been pretty high, at least where the ceiling was. The next thing he came around in his hospital bed in the ward.

He told us later on about what had happened. What he told us was something he couldn't have made up. He was never in that room before. He would never even have known about that room. He was in the main ward, on a monitor to count your heartbeats. Next thing he was being brought to this small room. He was unconscious at the time he was brought in and he woke up later in the bed he had gone to sleep in back in the ward. He would never have seen the room on the way in or on the way out. Yet he described it all so well.

I worked in the Belfast City Hospital at the time so I know that what he said was true. Everything tallies. I knew every part of the place. It was just a small room that you are taken into if you have a heart condition. They had all of the instruments and drugs there to bring you back should you go. They had adrenaline there that they used to stick into your heart. They had the pads, although things wouldn't have been as advanced then as they are now.

They would also have had the doctor who was on that night plus a couple of others. The only thing was my dad thought he was on a table but I think he was more likely on a trolley. They would have pushed him in there on a trolley. They would have whisked him in there as quickly as they could. The bed from the ward would have been too big to push down the corridor.

The doctors later confirmed he had actually died. Later still, in 1985, he actually did die at the age of 67. He knew then it was going to happen. The night before he died, he hadn't shaved – and he always shaved. He said to me, 'Look after your mother.'

It makes me wonder what is ahead of us. I'm Protestant although religion didn't mean very much to us when I was brought up. I believe in God but I really am a non-practising Protestant who has faith. Yet I think there is a soul and I've got a faith in God.

I think there is a life after death although I don't know what happens to your consciousness after you pass on. We won't know, I suppose, until we are at that point when we are facing God or moving on into another body or whatever. Sometimes I wonder is this a practice for the next bit? Are we going to move on and take up a new life somewhere else?

What happened to my dad certainly makes me wonder, 'Where do we go from here?'

KEVIN HILL, WHO LIVES IN COUNTY KERRY, had several out-of-body experiences while growing up in a London suburb.

When I was young, about 13 or 14, it started happening. Invariably I would be lying in bed, wanting to go to sleep but I wouldn't be able to. I would start to shudder. This shuddering, or vibration, was entirely within my brain or mind and didn't extend to my entire body. It was like as if my spirit was vibrating in order to exit my body. It was pointless resisting it and it occurred always of its own volition.

My bedroom was in a bungalow on the outskirts of London. The window looked out over the back garden. The room was decorated blue and I was in a single bed. It was a smallish bedroom and my parents' bedroom was next door, with an interconnecting door. They'd probably be in the living-room when this would be occurring. It would usually be dark. I'd be lying on the bed, wanting to go to sleep when this shuddering thing would start.

My person, or whatever it was, would then come out of my body and go up to the ceiling. I'd turn around and look down at myself. The real me was the one up above although I was looking down at a functioning, breathing body. But the body below was bereft of any spirit because I was the spirit. The first time it happened to me it was very upsetting. I thought I had died but I hadn't. Instead, after seconds rather than minutes, I was suddenly sucked back down again and re-entered the body.

This happened time and time again. I was very frightened the first time it happened and I was probably quite frightened the second time, but as it progressed I got quite used to it.

Sometimes it was a nuisance because really what I wanted to do was go to sleep and I was unable to. Initially I tried to resist it but it was hard to resist. It was insisting on happening.

I became so confident that I could eventually move further away from my body. I could fly out the window. The window would be closed. I'd be able to go out through it. I'd fly around the back garden, which I did on a few occasions. I would be travelling at a medium speed although I could have varied the speed according to what I wanted. It was a long garden and there was a river down at the end of it. It was probably close on 200 feet long. But it was short enough, in relative terms, so that I only needed to travel at medium pace.

I'd fly down to the end of the garden, where there was a conker tree. I'd be flying horizontal to the ground, face downwards. I wouldn't be that high up, just a few feet above the ground, not as high as the conker tree. I could put my head up and look around. Ironically I was always frightened of heights.

I'd come to the shallow river and I'd be able to fly up and down over it. I could feel the wind and hear the river rippling. I could see and hear the water. I could smell the water too. All my senses were available to me. I'd have a perspective that I never had of the river before. That was intriguing.

I might do this for 30 seconds or a minute and then I'd fly back in the window. I would fly over the bed and I'd be looking down at myself lying there. Within a couple of seconds I'd be back into the body again. There was no pain at all – I was just back in. I'd then roll over and go to sleep, sometimes grateful that it was over.

It was all quite enjoyable and a lot of fun. I felt I could go anywhere. I could do it at will. I felt I could fly anywhere in the world but there was always this nervousness inside me that if my body was moved I wouldn't be able to get back in again. I had the worry that if my mother came into the room and moved me that I might not be able to return. I was tempted to fly off to wherever but I didn't because I was too afraid, so I would only do it for a short time.

These experiences went on for maybe a year or two years and then they just ceased. They never happened again in my adult life, yet they were so vivid that I remember them clearly nearly 50 years later. I told a friend at school, who reckoned that he had a similar, although not identical, experience. I think he only had it once. I also told one or two people during my lifetime but I'm inclined not to because people might think you are bonkers. And I never told my parents. I wouldn't have dreamt of it.

I have thought about the possible religious ramifications of my out-of-body experiences but I am not convinced there are any. Although I was out of my body and flying around the back garden, I was still within our space and our time. I did not feel I had entered an alternative reality. I was certainly the same person. Yet I have often wondered, 'Is this the soul?' Was it my soul that came out and flew down the garden?

Or was it all dreams? I know when I have had a dream and it wasn't like that. If it was all dreams then why did I leave my body behind? In a dream I would have taken it with me. I have never had a dream where I have left my body behind and I doubt if anyone has. This was reality and it wasn't at all like a dream.

There must be a reason. I would toy with the idea that evolution grinds away largely unnoticed and my seemingly unnatural experiences may be perfectly natural and become increasingly common until at some time in the history of our species they are the norm. Whatever they were, they were absolutely amazing and I wish I could do them all over again.

CELIA, WHO LIVES IN COUNTY CLARE but who is originally from County Mayo, undertook what may well have been an out-of-body journey back in the late 1980s.

I was in my mid-20s and working in London at the time. I had a sister there and four brothers and we were all living in the same house. One night I went to bed as usual. I hadn't been out. I hadn't been drinking or anything like that. I hadn't been sick. I just went up to my room, which I shared with my sister. She was in a single bed by the window and I was by the other side.

I had a dream or sensation that I was travelling through the London Underground. I used it to get to work every day so it was familiar to me. It was dark and I was flying through it face downwards, just like an airplane. I was going through this long, dark space. I was going through the centre of the space, with my hands out. I wasn't frightened although I don't like the Underground. It didn't last very long, maybe seconds.

Next thing I had flown to Mayo and was over my parents' farm. I was hovering above the garden. I was just floating there. The garden was so real, as if I was there in reality. It was exactly as it always was. The house was there, the walls, the outhouses, the shed that my dad had the hay and turf in. I really felt I was at home.

My three youngest brothers were standing directly below me and wanted me to come down. Two of them were twins and there was another brother as well. They were trying to drag at my legs. They just couldn't reach me, even though the twins were quite tall. I couldn't go down to them although I wanted to, and they couldn't quite get me. That lasted a lot longer than my travel through the tunnel. Then I woke up.

I woke up with my legs in the air and I couldn't bring them down for about five minutes. I just couldn't do it. They were completely stiff and heavy, like they were paralysed. They were both kind of stuck together. I couldn't feel them. I did eventually get them down and I was thinking, 'What has just happened?' I was wondering whether I had travelled that night or was it just a dream.

Every now and again I still think about what happened. When I read stories or things in books about astral travel I wonder, 'Did that happen to me?' I am certain it wasn't the same as a dream. You know when you have had a dream and I do have weird dreams but this was different. It was just more real. To me it was more like travel than a dream. And I do think I travelled that night.

ELIZABETH, FROM COUNTY DOWN, felt herself leaving her body while settling down for a night's sleep.

I was up in my bedroom one night-time and I was in bed. I wasn't ill or anything. I was just lying down on my own but I wasn't asleep. I felt myself leaving my body and looking down and thinking, 'There I am below me. That's just the packaging. But it's not me. I'm here.'

I felt I was leaving my body completely and moving off. I was floating up above myself. I could see myself clearly below but I knew the real me was the one above and it was just a body down below. I thought, 'This is weird. I don't like this. I'm going to die. I'm about to go.' I felt if I went too much further I would be separated totally, probably dead.

It was all very real. I thought, 'I'm dying but I want to return.' I desperately wanted to come back. I can remember thinking, 'I must call for my husband.' He was downstairs. As I did, my voice came out very low, very slow and very deep. It felt very weird. I sounded like a man. I thought, 'Let me get back.' So he came up and I got back again. I was nervous and frightened about it. I didn't particularly want to believe I had separated spirit and body. But that is what I felt – that I'd left my body.

Eventually I told people and their reactions usually were, 'She's daft.' I remember, one time, one of my friends said to me, 'If I had a body like yours, I would leave it too.' She was being very funny. Most people don't believe you and I don't think it's a very believable thing unless you've experienced it. Yet strange things certainly happen.

One time I was talking in a small group and I recounted what happened to a very nice rector where I live. I'm Church of Ireland and I do go to church. He said, 'That's a real experience.' He didn't discount it at all as being silly talk. I've also since read books on out-of-body experiences and it was very much what I was experiencing at that time. But I actually stopped reading those books because I thought, 'Maybe I'm not doing the right thing. Maybe this is dangerous.'

A short time ago I was talking to a yoga teacher and, after telling her what happened, she said, 'That's very interesting. Would you like to come and join my yoga class? I do meditation.' I was definitely very interested. So I did yoga for quite a while and I developed an interest in deep meditation. But I got nervous of it because, at one particular time, I had this very strong feeling of three monks, in brown capes, standing there with their backs to me. They turned around and had empty, skeletal heads.

It wasn't a very nice experience. I am an artist and quite arty and I wondered whether something in my personality triggered it off. My teacher at the time said, 'Don't do it anymore on your own. You're leaving yourself open to the wrong sort of spiritual experience.' So I stopped doing yoga. And I haven't felt it since.

Perhaps as an artist it is possible that when I left my body I was just having fanciful thoughts. Maybe that was just the arty side coming out of me, in imagination. It could be associated with deep relaxation. Maybe I was just so deeply relaxing my body that it happened. Yet it still felt very real. I think the real me was the one looking down on the body and the body itself was of no real importance. It certainly felt very real and I felt it very much.

BRENDAN, FROM COUNTY KERRY, practised how to travel outside of his body. As was mentioned in the introduction to this chapter, the techniques of out-of-body travel can be learned.

I started trying it about ten years ago. I tried it first out of curiosity. I read about it because, at the time, I was very much into looking for knowledge or truth. I found a great book called *The Projection Of The Astral Body*, which was by Sylvan Muldoon and Hereward Carrington. It was a hard-cover book and it came out I suppose 80 years ago. They researched it well. All the techniques were there. That's how it started.

The key thing is relaxation and to let your muscles go limp. You have to be totally relaxed, which is very hard to do. You also have to be totally focused and concentrate on going out. Breathing has a lot to do with it too. You have to breathe in a certain fashion – slow and deep. I would call it the 'breath of relaxation.' But the most important factor is to believe that you are going to do it. That's a very hard thing. You have to more or less hypnotise yourself into believing that it's possible and that you will succeed.

I did it about five or six times. The first experience was very strange. I did it lying down in bed. I kept trying and the next thing I felt was that I was shrinking. I felt my feet were moving up towards my head. My other body was contracting into a sort of a point. I had a strange feeling in my body. I could hear a sound like a jet engine, like a 'fluffing' sound in my ears. It got louder and louder. I felt as if I was ballooning, as if there was an expansion within my body, as if something was going out of me.

All of a sudden I found myself in a different place. I found myself inside a house, looking out of a window. I don't know where it was, somewhere in the countryside. I could see tiles on the floor and the greenery outside and the trees. The colour was spectacular. The colours that we see every day are dead by comparison. I was conscious of myself being out of my body although I wasn't conscious of the body I left behind.

The second time I found myself standing under a huge wall. It was an eight-foot or ten-foot high wall. I don't know where it was. I don't know why I was there. All of a sudden there were pebbles on top of this wall. They dropped down to the ground. The strange thing about it was that the sound they made when they hopped off the ground was a kind of a hollow, melodic sound. It was an artificial sound, very pure, like a hollow echo.

That time I found it hard to get back to my physical body. My whole body was paralysed. I couldn't move a muscle. I had no power over it at all. That scared me. The only way I could get out of it was to rock my head from side to side and keep rocking it. That way I was able to get the muscles going again. They call it a cataleptic trance. But it didn't feel like a trance, which I always thought was a hazy stupor. This was real.

I tried it another time during the day. This time I left my body and found myself trying to switch on the light. It was a bit darkish, in the early evening. My finger kept slipping off the switch. I don't know whether my finger was slipping off it or going through it. I just couldn't put on the light. Then, for some strange reason, I knew that my wife was lighting the fire below in the sitting-room. I confirmed afterwards that she was.

That time I had a problem getting back into my body. I didn't get in right. The two bodies got entangled. I could feel the elbow of my physical body up against the chin of let's call it my psychic body. My arm got wrapped around my psychic body. I was in a real quandary and couldn't disentangle myself. I just relaxed and somehow shifted myself around a bit. I was grand after that.

It can happen that people worry they won't find their body again. I was always scared that I mightn't be able to come back and I might be buried alive or something. I worried that I might be caught outside and they might think my physical body was dead. No one would realise that I was actually somewhere else. That was a big fear with me.

I gave it up because I had a bad experience. One night I was in this pitch-black place, a space of blackness. All of a sudden these demonic heads came rushing at me. I became afraid. Another reason I gave it up was because my alternative body became too loose for my physical body. Sometimes I felt myself going off without wanting to. That frightened me.

I worried especially when I was driving a car. I thought I would be dangerous to both myself and the public. I wondered what would happen if I left myself – who would be driving the car? That really scared me when I was driving along the road because I thought I might lose control of the car.

I believe anybody can do it. If I can do it, anybody can do it. It's a bit like riding a bicycle. When you first ride a bicycle, you can't imagine how you are going to do it. You wonder,

'How am I going to balance on two wheels?' You find it difficult at first but once you get the knack of it, it's easy. And the experience is very real.

I think there's another side to us all that lurks beneath the surface. I really think there is a 'spirit' side. I don't like using that word but it's probably the best way of describing it. I think we evolved from some source way back before we were physical. It might have been some sort of vibration. All creation is energy vibration. Whatever it was, it is still in us.

I think we have many layers. The outer layer is the physical one but there's an inner one as well. There might be an even purer one within that again, with its own reality. All the old sages, long ago, said that everything has seven layers, seven bodies if you like. I kind of believe that.

VISIONS AND VISITATIONS

Irish author and playwright Hugh Leonard had a visit from his deceased wife shortly after her death. The couple, who were married for 45 years, had been close. 'When she went, the house was empty,' Leonard said of his Belgian wife Paule, who passed away in 2000. 'There was one day I sat here at the typewriter and I cried for ten hours. I was doing solitaire on the computer and in ten hours I didn't win a game. It was just as if nothing would work for me.'

Paule's visitation happened about eight months after her death. Leonard – whose real name was John Keyes Byrne and who later died in 2009 – was working upstairs in his home. He needed some information which was contained in a small pile of newspapers on the floor below. He walked downstairs quickly, his mind preoccupied with the work he was doing. He entered the living-room and was startled by what he saw.

'I walked into the living-room and she was standing facing the fireplace,' the author recalled. She was in her dressing-gown, with her hair like gold. 'Before I could blink she was gone. It was as if I had caught her when she didn't mean to be caught. I can tell you what she was wearing. I can tell you exactly the turn of her head, absolutely everything. She was there, solid as anything, and then just went.'

The experience, Leonard said later, was vivid and not an illusion. It gave him a new-found perspective on life after death: 'I just know that what we're in now is a kind of a stage, but I think there is definitely a continuation and in that sense there's a meaning. God has nothing to do with this. We have got to make a difference between God and the continuation after death. One doesn't necessarily mean there's another.'

Visions, according to the dictionary, are the experience of seeing, as if with the eyes, either the supernatural or supernatural beings. Although mystical and surreal, they are common. Reports of ghosts, spirits, poltergeists, banshees and many other shadowy and ethereal figures have littered Irish history from the time of the Celts.

Irish literature and poetry are riddled with dark tales of hauntings and spectral appearances. They have been written by authors including Bram Stoker, James Stephens, Lady Gregory, W. B. Yeats, Joseph Sheridan Le Fanu and Oscar Wilde. This section of the book, however, is concerned with something quite different.

Three categories of visions form the bulk of the following chapter. One category involves visitations shortly after death. In such cases it is often claimed that souls come back to reassure relatives that the deceased are happy and doing well. It is also argued that the souls return because they are lost on their journeys to the otherworld or are in a transitory stage in between lives. These souls, it is additionally claimed, may belong to people who die suddenly or unexpectedly and therefore struggle to find their way to the light.

The second category involves what many believe to be spirits returning to help the living in times of urgent need. Most involve the appearance of deceased family members, such as parents, husbands or wives. The third and final category consists of visions of the afterlife or future events. Such visions have been chronicled since long before Biblical times and are still widely reported.

Sceptics might argue that since visions in all three categories frequently occur before or after sleep, they are really subconscious dreams and not real. Afterlife proponents, to the contrary, say that because people are relaxed and at ease around sleep then their senses are more open and receptive to experiencing them.

In the case of visitations, many occur in the upper left corner of the room. For example, Ethna, who is interviewed later, describes how her father, following his death, visited her on half a dozen occasions over three months always in the upper left corner of the room. 'He appeared in the corner of the bedroom, near a window,' she explains with clear recall. 'It was the left-hand corner, as you looked out from the bed.'

Ethna's observation accords with the conclusions of the eminent researcher P. M. H. Atwater who reported that the majority of similar cases she studied in America occupied the upper left corner of a room. Only a few occupied the right side, and virtually all were in a ceiling corner.

The news imparted by those who return is mostly good. Few come back in distress although unhappy experiences are sometimes reported. One story in this chapter describes a disturbing afterlife vision where 'millions and millions' of bodies climb under and over each other through mud, rising and falling in unison as they repeat the gruesome procedure over and over again.

Interestingly, similar images of pulsating, rhythmic activities appear in ancient texts. One text describes how an otherworld traveller witnessed 'globes of dusky flame' rising rhythmically from a great pit and falling back down again, each globe filled with condemned souls. The globes are constantly tossed up and down from the pit.

Another text, which originates in fifteenth century France, describes the damned repeatedly scurrying back and forth between blasts of icy wind and a frozen flood. The pattern is replicated time and again. Yet another text describes the condemned with their faces turned behind them, marching painfully and slowly in a circle. Monotonous repetition of mundane and often horrifying routines clearly forms part of the negative vision experience.

In the main, however, the impact of visions is usually said to be calming and reassuring. Those who experience them are comforted by being reacquainted with the form, thoughts, moods, memories and sensations of those who have passed away. They are heartened that their loved ones are safe. As it happens, virtually all of the following narratives had a positive impact, beginning with a story from Munster.

MARY LYNCH, FROM COUNTY CORK, had a visit from her recently-deceased father as she battled for life following an accident. She was aged 15 at the time.

In November 2000 my father died of an aneurysm. He was only 49. It was a terrible shock. He was in fine health although he did feel sick for about two weeks beforehand. He never really told us because he hated having anyone else worrying.

All of a sudden he got this aneurysm. It happened on a Sunday and he died on a Thursday. There were four of us and my mom in the family. It was devastating. Even our dog died afterwards. They told us he probably died of a broken heart.

I was in my Junior Cert. year at the time. I remember, one day, being out with my mom in the car and she started crying and said to me, 'I just don't know why he had to die.' I said, 'It was probably to protect us from something worse happening.' We didn't think much about that comment, never knowing what was going to happen next.

About 11 weeks after my father had died, I was up in my friend's house with my sister. My mom rang and said that my sister had to go to piano lessons. She asked me, 'Would you be able to walk down with her?' I said, 'I'll do it.' So we walked down with my friend and we passed the bus station.

I saw a bus driver who I knew from bringing me to school. He was parked in a bus. We ran across the road and said hello to him. It was kind of a lane, or a small road, next to the bus station. He opened the driver's window. I stood there talking to him.

Another bus came along and I was caught between the two buses. I only remember bits of it but I remember being pushed in. I was crushed. The driver I was talking to was screaming to the other guy to keep moving because I was stuck. I think my leg got caught on the side of the tyre so I got turned around and pushed in again.

I was pulled along for a bit and then I fell onto the ground in front of the bus that was parked. I was conscious. I thought I felt fine for a minute. I went to get up but all I could move was my left shoulder. The first thought I had was, 'Oh, no! I bet I have broken some bones. I hope I'm only in hospital for the weekend because I have school on Monday and I don't want to be breaking my attendance.' Then, all of a sudden, a searing pain came up from my toes. It went straight up, right through me. I was in agony at that stage.

I could feel the pain getting worse and I couldn't breathe properly. I was vomiting blood. I asked would they roll me over. A lady who was there helped me and grabbed my right arm and she rolled me over. Didn't my hip break! I had crushed my pelvic bone. I said, 'Roll me back again.' I had got an awful fright when I heard the crack. So they rolled me back again. I could feel the blood foaming in my mouth. I felt myself losing consciousness but I kept my eyes open. I didn't know what to do.

Suddenly, as plain as day, my father came up to me. He was in amongst the crowd. He looked like he was only 27, 28 or 29. He looked so young. I had never seen him at that age because I wasn't alive then. He had his Sunday clothes on and he was smiling. He always had a huge gap in his teeth and I recognised him as he was smiling at me.

He had his green jumper on and a check patterned pants with bits of green in it, which I recognised. Every time I remember him when I was young he had grey hair because he was going grey, but his hair was dark brown that day. His skin was younger. He was so real.

He came over to me and asked me, 'Are you alright?' I said, 'No. I'm not.' I said, 'I can't breathe. I just can't breathe. What am I going to do?' I was trying to explain to him that I couldn't breathe and I was panicking because I couldn't. He said to me, 'You'll be OK. You'll be fine. Take it easy and calm down now. You'll be fine. You'll be OK.' He just stood over me and didn't touch me. He was so soothing. He was always like that anyway. So I relaxed a bit.

I had forgotten that he was dead. I thought he was alive and had just arrived. I thought he was there as a person. I knew he was there because I saw him plain as day. I thought he was after coming in from town or something. I just didn't know. It wasn't until later, in the ambulance, that I thought, 'My God! Dad is dead!'

The next thing I remember was they put me on a stretcher and put me into the ambulance. I got into hospital and I was brought into the resuscitation room. They were saying that usually after people come in with crush injuries they are definitely unconscious or dead or near-dead. They said it was so unusual that I was talking to them about holidays and everything like that.

I was actually kind of hard on them as well because, when I was lying on the stretcher and they were cutting off my clothes, I looked over and I saw the other side of the room and I said, 'My father died here 11 weeks ago.' One of the nurses started crying. She remembered it and she remembered us.

I also remembered that when my father died they put the jewellery he was wearing into a bag and handed it to my mom and she fell apart when she got it. They were putting my jewellery into a bag and I said to them, 'Don't do that because my mom is going to think I'm not going to be OK. Go out and tell her that I'm grand and there's nothing wrong with me.'

This was a Friday evening and they said to my mom, 'She's going to be dead by Sunday.' My left ear had been torn off. I had crushed all the bones in my right arm. I had torn my liver in six places. I had crushed my pelvis. I had a head injury but I don't think that was as severe. I had torn open my leg as well and they were going to do skin-grafts on that although luckily they didn't have to.

They told my mom, 'Look, we are not going to put her into Intensive Care because we need the bed for somebody who has a better chance. We will put her into another room and the nurses will take care of her until she dies. There's nothing we can do. We've given her blood but it's coming straight back out again. All we can do is give her oxygen and keep her going.'

My mom later told me that, after being told that I was going to die, she stood out in the hall praying. She then came in to see me. I said, 'Come around. I can't see you.' My head was swollen and I couldn't see out of my right eye. So she came around to my left side. I could see the tears in her eyes. I said, 'It's fine. Dad was there and he said it is going to be fine.' She said, 'Oh!' She later said that at the time she didn't take it seriously because I had such a huge trauma. She didn't believe it.

By Sunday I was still alive and they said, 'She's pulling through so far but we'll have to sew up her stitches because it is 48 hours and she'll catch infections.' I was anointed by that stage and they brought my friends in to say goodbye to me although they didn't want me to know I was dying. They came in and they were saying, 'Good luck in the operation.'

My mom also wished me luck but she wouldn't stay because she was too upset about the whole thing. They said to her, 'That's probably it, really.' So she left and they brought me into theatre. They put me under anaesthetic. I remember them putting me out and I remember being still awake after I counted up to ten. So they turned up the gas and I was asleep within seconds.

My mom later told me that after the operation I was taken back into Intensive Care again. Obviously I had survived. The surgeon came back out to my mom and said, 'I want to say this off the record – her heart stabilised under the anaesthetic. It was like there was somebody watching over her. I don't know what happened but she shouldn't be alive. I can't say this to you on the record but off the record there's a miracle after happening and she's definitely going to live.' My mom didn't know what to say.

When my mom came in to me again, I asked her, 'Did I tell you I saw my dad at the accident?' She said, 'You did. What did you mean by that?' I told her what had happened. She sat there and she said she knew then that it truly was a miracle, that something spectacular and out of the ordinary had happened. She knew herself; she could feel there was something.

I absolutely know it was my dad that day. He certainly walked out of the crowd. I know myself it was him. It was his voice. He was always so gentle and everything. I knew my dad and how he used to talk to me and calm me down. I had been so close to him. It also wasn't like I was looking for him at the accident; my sister had been next to me and she told me my mom was on her way. It is truly amazing.

I feel he is still with me. I feel I'm protected in some way. I don't take advantage of it but I always feel that there's something there with me. It's not like I feel a presence but I feel so safe in myself. Even on certain occasions where things happen to me that I feel are going against me, they actually turn out to be the best things ever.

I would have always thought it was coincidence. But when I look back on my accident and my father dying, and everything that happened, I feel it's different. I do believe there is something watching me. I feel protected. I count my blessings. I thank God for it and know it was obviously meant to be.

JACK HYNES, FROM COUNTY CLARE, was visited by his deceased mother one night in 2005. The visit occurred after he awoke from his sleep with pains in his chest. Her advice saved his life.

I went to bed on 17 January 2005. It was just six months or so before my fiftieth birthday. I live on my own and I had been out with the dogs that day. I bring them up to a wood. When I was coming out of the wood I felt a bit of a wobble. I didn't think much of it because I had been out for an extra-long walk and I thought it was a bit of tiredness. I felt great, went home and had my dinner, sat down, read the paper and watched a bit of television, did the usual Sunday evening kind of thing.

I went to bed around 11 or 11.30 but I woke up around 2 o'clock. I felt I had very severe indigestion down the chest area, towards the stomach. I went downstairs and took a Nurofen painkiller but it made no difference. It just got worse. I came back upstairs and I felt the pain going out onto my left shoulder and going down along my arm. I thought, 'This is strange.' But the possibility of a heart attack never hit me. I felt totally in control.

When I came back upstairs I leaned on the dressing-table. I put my hands on it. I was sort of holding myself, with my arms out in front of me. I looked in the mirror. Even though it was dark I could see this greyness by the top right-hand side of the mirror. It was over the reflection of my shoulder. It was like the image of a face and it was looking back at me. It was my deceased mother.

She was talking to me and said, 'This is not a pain in your stomach or indigestion. There's something worse here.' She was saying, 'Come on! Get yourself going!' I could hear her voice in my ear. She was a soft-spoken woman. It was the same voice she had when she died – a 72-year-old voice – with her West Clare accent. It was definitely her and she was concerned. She had a serious tone.

I lay down on the bed again but the voice came to me once more. There was something in my ear saying, 'Don't lie down! Come on! Get yourself moving! Get to hospital!' I couldn't sleep it off. She just kept at me. I felt that mobility was somehow very important; I had to keep moving. I made an effort to lie down three times but there was no way I was being let do it. I kept hearing, 'Come on! Come on! Get going!' I could really feel my mother's presence, without a doubt.

Eventually I put on a pullover and a pair of jeans and my runners without my socks. I went over to the hospital, which wasn't far away. I felt she was with me during the drive. I went into Casualty. The doctor gave me a morphine injection, which kind of knocked me out. I was brought up into Intensive Care and I was in hospital for two weeks after that, on monitors.

I remember, the following day, the Intensive Care nurse came over to my bed and said, 'What do you think you had?' I said, 'It felt like severe indigestion.' I will never forget her response. There were no ifs or buts about her. She said, 'You had no indigestion. You had a heart attack.' The way she said it shook me. Apparently it was touch-and-go for a while. Being 50 was a milestone and I thought, 'God! I hope I'm going to see my fiftieth birthday.'

I had to get an angiogram done, which showed up a blockage on the back area of the heart. The doctor had to go in three times with the wire that goes up through you. I had been told it would only take 20 minutes. But I was in there for an hour-and-a-half. I was under a local anaesthetic. The nurse afterwards came over and said, 'He tried his best.' That was her exact statement. Straight away I thought I was going to have to go to Dublin for a bypass.

The doctor later explained, 'We had a small problem because the blockage was on a bend so I couldn't get the stent in. But we dilated it out, blew it out.' I said, 'Were you happy with that?' He said, 'I'm pretty happy alright.' I felt, 'If you're happy, I'm happy.' It was a wake-up call and I changed my diet dramatically. I've lost weight. I go to the gym three times a week. I walk the dogs. I play squash and I'm feeling fine ever since.

I'm certain it was my mother, 100 per cent. She was the old-type mother that would never let you down. She was always the one you could go to. She'd be the one that would always put your mind at rest over things. She was a very calm woman herself but she was trying to get me to move as quick as I could. I believe she saw what was happening and tried to get me moving.

The fact that she never let me feel it was a heart attack was typically her. She knew that if I felt it was a heart attack I would have panicked. It would probably have made things worse. All she was saying was, 'Go to the hospital and get a more qualified opinion.'

Even when I lay down and tried to sleep I felt she, like many mothers, was trying to nag, nag, nag. I could have nodded off and that might have been it. I might never have woken up again. The fact that it wasn't the pain that woke me but that I just woke up out of my sleep makes me believe it was her. If I had fallen asleep I would now be a statistic rather than an actual person.

As a result, I always feel my parents are with me. When I go into the graveyard where they are buried I always chat to them. It's not prayers that I say, just a chat. I might even talk sport to my father, if Clare are playing. My mother loved music and I talk to her about that. I owe her a lot and I feel she is very much around. If ever there is a problem, I look to her. She advises me still to this day.

BERNIE, FROM COUNTY DUBLIN, met her deceased son shortly after she mysteriously collapsed in 2007.

I was going down the street where I live. I started walking as if I was drunk yet I don't drink. I kept on going although I felt funny. There was a seat on the street outside this shop. I sat on it. My friend, Marion, owned the shop. She came out to me and said, 'Bernie, what's wrong?' I said, 'I don't know but

I don't feel too good.' She brought me into the shop and got me a glass of water. She rang my doctor and he sent for an ambulance.

When I was in the ambulance, I was coming in and out of consciousness. I was lying down flat. They had an oxygen mask on my face. Marion had come with me and she was there along with the driver and the paramedic. Suddenly they were banging my chest. I had no pulse. They were trying to resuscitate me. I knew they were doing it but I really felt I wasn't there. I was pronounced dead. They said to Marion, 'She's gone!'

The next thing I saw my son Alan, who had died in 1981. He was just five-and-a-half when he died. A bin lorry reversed over him. He had been a big fan of the programme *CHiPs*, which was a cop show. He and his brother were mad into that. He had the *CHiPs* uniform, which I had got him, and we buried him in it. He was wearing that when I saw him.

There was like a star behind his head. It wasn't like a halo. It was like in the shape of icicles coming out of his head. It was glowing so bright. His head had been crushed under the bin lorry but he had no scars, no bandages – nothing. There was also like a big light beyond him. It was so bright. I could see it way in the distance.

He was right beside me, just the way he was at five-and-a-half. The only difference was this big glow around him. He said nothing. His hands were down straight by his side. There was nobody with him. It was so peaceful. He was on his own. He just smiled as if to say, 'Mam, I'm OK.'

I was delighted he was there. I thought, 'I'm going to see him! I'm going to him! This is it! This is it!' After he passed away I lived to die so that I could be with him. I was oblivious to everything else. Now I was going to Alan. But he wasn't reaching out to me. A neighbour who is older than I am later said to me, 'When he hadn't got his hands out, he wasn't reaching for you. It wasn't your time to go.'

He then just disappeared. I later learned that the time when I had seen him, with the big light behind him, was the time when I was pronounced dead. I know that because my friend Marion heard me say, 'I see Alan! Bye!' She later told me that was when they said, 'She's gone!'

I ended up in the hospital and my family were sent for. I remember my daughter was hitting my face. Somebody was screaming, 'Wake up! Wake up!' They were saying, 'Open your eyes! Open your eyes!' I could hear them but I wasn't there. I didn't feel anything. I didn't feel any of the slaps, yet when I woke up later my chest was bruised as if a tractor had run over it.

All of a sudden I was alright. It was as if nothing had happened. I could remember being wonky going down the street but I didn't know I had been pronounced dead. I didn't find that out until later. I didn't feel there was anything wrong. They did tests – ECGs, heart tests, the lot – and nothing showed up. I was only in hospital for about three days and they couldn't find anything. I've been fine ever since.

It was a beautiful vision and it gave me an inner strength. You know the way they say, 'Part of me went with you when God called you home.' Well my heart broke when I lost Alan. But this gave me a new outlook and a stronger faith.

I know now he's alright. I know he's waiting for me. He has my seat ready up there. I know there is a life after death. To me, this is hell. The place we go to is heaven, with all the happiness and the glow. I know that's where we will go and, as they say, the chain will get its links all together.

PHILOMENA, FROM COUNTY KERRY, lost her daughter in a tragic accident and, many years later, her husband through a heart attack. The vision that her husband saw prior to his death was quite remarkable.

We lost our daughter Patricia, who was drowned in 1968. We were living in England at the time. She was 12-and-a-half years old and a dote of a girl. She was one of the most innocent girls you could ever meet. She never believed there was any wrong in anybody.

She studied in the school where I was teaching. In her final year, however, she went to grammar school. She would come home in the evening and she would be telling me stories she heard from people she met on the bus. I used to say to her, 'Patricia, you be careful, you can't really talk that freely to strangers.' She always reassured me. After she died, letters poured in from the people she had met on the bus.

What happened was that Patricia was on a school outing, a school trip down to Hastings. She was terrified of the water. She couldn't swim. Dad wouldn't allow her to go because of that. She was so disappointed. We were at breakfast on that last morning when she had to have the news in whether she could or couldn't go. Her dad asked her, 'How many are not going?' She said, 'Dada, I'm the only one not allowed to go.' He was always 'Dada'. John said, 'Oh, we can't have that.' So she went.

That evening a policeman arrived. We had just got in. We had been visiting my brother and sister-in-law, who lived not very far away from us. John was only closing the door when I saw the policeman coming up the steps. I said, 'John, don't close the door, there's a policeman coming.' It never dawned on me. But the first thing John said was, 'Is it Patricia?' The next thing he said was, 'Is she dead?' I said, 'John, don't ask that question.' But the policeman said, 'She is.'

It turned out that down in Hastings, because she couldn't swim, she was only paddling. A freak wave came in. There was a detective walking his dog on the cliff. He risked his life to get down to her and try to save her. He resuscitated her. That came out in the inquest.

I couldn't talk to God for the whole week after she died. I was completely insane. All I could say to him was, 'We always prayed. We always did what we should have done. And now you have taken our child. How can you possibly do that to people that you love?' I wouldn't go to mass and I'm a daily mass-goer. I just couldn't go. All I could say was, 'How can I go and pretend to God that what he has done is alright.' But we did go to mass eventually and it really did something for me.

I was dreading going back to school. But I went back and I was teaching children that had grown up with Patricia. They knew her, of course, and they were all great friends. They thought it was terrible. Lots of letters had poured in from their parents.

I always gave the children a free period on Friday afternoon. The children used to talk during that period. The first question one of my pupils, Sally Anne, asked was, 'If God loves us how can he send some people such heavy crosses?' I wasn't in a position to answer that. I was still not 100 per cent sure. But another child, Marie, shot up: 'Can I answer that question for you?' I said, 'Do, please, Marie.' And she said, 'I'm just surprised at Sally Anne asking that question. Doesn't she know that God knows us and he knows what each of us can carry?'

We were devastated. Patricia was the first girl in the family, the oldest. Her dad thought there was nothing like her. There were two other daughters, Geraldine and Dolores, who were absolutely wonderful. They used to write notes, which would be on the breakfast table every morning and they reassured us they were praying. But her dad was broken-hearted. Everyone used to say, 'How will John cope?' It was the same thing that often dawned on me. I think I had to be very practical.

Then, in 1992, it was obvious my husband was dying. He had trouble with his heart, among other things. However, we decided to go on holiday over to England, near where we had originally lived. Our daughter Dolores was over there with her husband, who was working on a big project. Strangely, when we were leaving home here in Kerry, as I closed the kitchen door behind us a shiver went up my spine. I knew that John wouldn't be back.

After we got over, John wasn't well. We were only there not even two days when he had a bad heart attack. He was taken into hospital and we were told that he wouldn't survive and that he certainly wouldn't travel home again. He came back to Dolores' place on a Monday and he was very unwell. He was in a really big room, with a beautiful wooden bed.

All through the rest of that week he was talking with his father and mother, who had both passed away. The conversation was unbelievable. It was more or less, 'I'm fine. Are you alright?' It was all about Glin, in County Limerick, which was his home place. It was all so real.

He died on the Saturday. He had been downstairs for a cup of coffee and then we got him back up to bed. After a few minutes he said to me, 'Who is the lovely girl by my bed?' It was about 11 o'clock in the day. At this stage I didn't know how lucid he was so I pretended it was Dolores. But he said, 'Not at all, Phil. Dolores has gone downstairs long ago. Who is this beautiful blondie girl?' Dolores is dark but Patricia was fair. He only said it once. At that, his face lit up. He knew who it was.

He never mentioned her name. He never spoke to her. All he did was follow her around the room, with a smile on his face. That's all he did, all that time, was watch her. You knew that she was moving because he was following every move.

The expression on his face said it all. It gave me such comfort. He kept asking me, 'Phil, say another one of your prayers.' And he kept following her around the room. That went on until he died, that same evening, with me beside him holding his hand.

I could never describe the peace. I know Patricia was there. Even now, with them both gone, I never feel that they are far away. If I need them – if I'm down in the dumps, which isn't very often – the strength I get from Patricia and John is unbelievable.

I don't honestly know how anybody could cope in a circumstance like mine if they didn't believe. It would be so sad. I have no doubt in the world that we will all meet again. All I know is that Patricia and John will be waiting for me.

ARTHUR SPENCE, FROM BELFAST, had a vision of his father during the closing days of the Second World War. His dad was a sapper with the British Army and was posted to the Italian front. The vision proved to be tragically prophetic.

I was 15-and-a-half years old at the time. My father, who was also called Arthur, had joined the British Army and he was in the Royal Engineers as a sapper. He had always been a docker in Belfast and his job was to unload ships. As far as I know, he was at D-Day. My oldest brother was in the Navy and he was there too, although they never met on D-Day itself.

My dad went right through the whole war until he was

transferred into Italy. It was near the end of the war. We knew the war was almost over because we heard it from different people coming home. My mum had a letter saying that he was looking forward so much to coming home and that the Italian campaign was coming to an end. We were all looking forward to seeing him again.

One day a letter came to my mum, who was called Eliza Jane but who had the nickname 'Dodi'. She had, by the way, raised seven of a family – four boys and three girls. The postmen in those days were very friendly. They knew your first name and all that. He came to her and said, 'Dodi, there's a letter for you.' It was a War Office letter reporting that my dad was missing.

We waited for more news. I read the Bible and prayed that my dad would be found safe. I kept praying. I had got a job at the time as a lorry-boy in one of the oil companies. It was called the 'Pool' Board then, because all the oil companies had merged into one during the war. They were known as the Petroleum Board but they got 'Pool' for short.

One or two days after the letter arrived, I was up loading on the gantry where everything you'd touch was steel. I was helping load a tanker when all of a sudden I started to get electric shocks. The driver was concerned and he went and got the manager. The manager tried it but he didn't get any shocks.

Because everything was highly flammable the manager said, 'I'll have to close everything down.' He got the engineers and they did a complete check over five or six hours or more. Not one of them got a shock. Yet when I went back up again, I got more shocks. The manager said, 'I think you should go on home.'

That night I went to bed early. It was dusk at the time and there was a sort of brightness in the room. We had one light on the ceiling, with a 50-watt bulb which was lit. There were no shadows. My brother, who was in the Navy, was home on leave and there was just him and my mum down in the kitchen. I left them have time together, talking. I got into bed and kept praying that my father would be OK and safe.

I was lying there when, all of a sudden, I stopped praying and I looked up and saw my father standing at the bottom of the bed. My dad was clear as day. He had his khaki uniform on and his black beret that the Engineers wore. He was down at the bottom of the bed, by the iron bars. He was standing there. He hadn't a worried look on his face. He was just the loveable dad standing there as if to say, 'I've gone. I'm alright. Don't be worried.' It looked as if he wanted to touch. I froze solid. I couldn't move.

All of a sudden I let out an unmerciful yell. My brother came running up the stairs and he said, 'What is it?' I said, 'John, my dad is standing at the bottom of the bed.' John put his hand out and said, 'There's nobody there.' I could see my dad standing beside him. I could still see him. I said, 'John, he's standing right beside you.' But John said, 'He's not there. There's nobody there.' All of a sudden my dad started to disappear and he faded away.

The next morning, or the morning after, my mother got another official letter. The same postman came. My mother was down scrubbing our hall in our two-up, two-down house. She was always down on her knees, scrubbing the tile floors. The postman knew what the letter was. He said, 'Dodi, I have a letter for you.' My mum looked at the letter and the next thing she just squealed with shock. The postman couldn't stand it. He said, 'I'm sorry, Dodi' and walked off.

The letter said my father had been killed. I then told my mum about seeing my dad and she said, 'I don't know, son, but all things are possible with God.' I told her I had been praying for my dad's safe return. I told her about a part of the Bible I had read which says, 'Do not pray for those who are dead, because they have already passed over.' And I believe today that the Lord had sent my dad to say, 'Don't be praying, son. I've already gone from this scene of time.'

Later we learned how my father ended up in Bari, where his job was to offload ships in the harbour. There were American and British ships offloading there. I read a book which described how a German plane flew over the docks for two or three days and it wasn't intercepted. It must have been taking aerial photographs.

We also discovered that, one day, my father relieved one of his mates, to let him off. He was offloading a ship when this plane came over and dropped bombs. There were explosions in the ships. People tried to get away. Some of the ships did their best to get out of the harbour but others couldn't.

One of the ships they hit was the one my dad was offloading. My dad was a great swimmer but the ships were docked so tight to each other that he must have got jammed against the side of the ship. He was submerged. When they got him out, there was only one little mark across his forehead. He had drowned. He was only 42 and he died on 9 April 1945.

I look back on it with sorrow and disbelief. It was tragic because my dad was ready for coming back home and would soon have been demobbed. The German Army was in retreat. I thought no more were going to lose their lives but unfortunately my dad lost his. It's a sad story.

I have asked different people, different clergymen, to try and explain my dad's appearance to me. One minister said, 'It must have been the intervention of the Supreme God above, to show you to stop praying for your father because he had gone from this life.' I do honestly believe to this day that it was God's way of telling me that my father had passed from this scene of time into the other part of life.

DAVID DOHERTY, FROM DERRY, describes how he had a disturbing vision while in hospital for a heart operation.

Back in 2003 I was told I needed a triple bypass operation. I was sent to a hospital in Glasgow because I could get the bypass done quicker. I got the operation done and I was told I would be out in about nine days. But what happened was, rather than get better after the operation, I had a terrible pain in my chest and it wouldn't go away.

They did X-rays and said, 'Unfortunately you're going to have to go back into theatre.' Back in theatre they found that the sternum bone had all disintegrated after the first operation. It was taken away and they left me like that, hoping it would heal.

After about a week I was getting down and down and down. I was feeling worse, falling asleep and was still in the hospital. The next thing I was taken into Intensive Care. My wife asked, 'What's wrong?' The doctor said, 'He's a very sick man.' She said, 'How sick?' He said, 'I think you should get your family over.' So the family and friends all flew over from Derry. I went unconscious and I saw nothing for almost a month.

The first week, while I was unconscious, they told my wife, 'Look, he's very ill but we're going to see what we can do.' My kidneys were gone. My blood was poisoned. They kept trying different things all week to counteract the infection. Nothing was working. They ended up telling my wife, 'Things aren't going well here.'

They said, 'We're very sorry. We've tried everything we can. Nothing is working. There's nothing more we can do.'

They gave the impression that I was going to die soon. At one stage they expected that I would die in the next 12 hours. My son and my sister-in-law went home to get the house ready for bringing me back in a coffin and for a funeral.

When I was so near death, I had what I call a 'dream' – but it was much more than a dream, it was like I was living it. It wasn't vague, it was real. I thought I was dead. I honestly felt it was happening. I couldn't see myself but I could see everything around me.

I saw myself dead in a coffin, getting waked in a little village outside of Derry called Claudy. It's about a ten-minute drive away. I had been through the village before but it had no real meaning to me. It didn't mean anything special, only that my work would have taken me through it.

I was getting waked out in the open, in a green. There were seats all around, down both sides, for people to sit on. People were walking about. I was lying there. I could see them but I couldn't talk to them or communicate with them in any way. I couldn't identify anybody I knew. Although I was dead I could hear everybody moving around me.

They closed the coffin and carried me up the street to the main road out of Claudy. They put me on the back of the hearse to carry me back to Derry. It was just me and two people. One of them was a woman and a fellow was driving the hearse.

When I was in the hearse and while they were driving along, the 'dream' changed. All of a sudden I was standing in a field and I could see over the hills and mountains. I could see for miles and miles in all directions, right over the horizon. There was no colour, everything was black and white. There was no green or anything like that.

Everything was really gloomy. On the ground there was nothing but muck and millions and millions of bodies climbing under and over each other. It was like in formation – first under a body and then over a body, climbing through muck. It was like a grey mess, everything was covered in mud.

It was being communicated to me that that was what I was going to have to do – climb under a body and over a body. I was very distraught. I thought I was in hell or someplace, although we are led to believe that hell is all fire. I felt traumatised about what was happening to me.

I honestly felt it was happening. I was getting ready to do it. I saw a woman stand up, as if she was a supervisor in charge of these bodies. I only saw her from the back. The mud was dripping off her when she stood up. The woman was dressed but covered in mud. It was very vivid.

I thought to myself, 'Have I to do this forever? Am I someplace where this is me for the rest of eternity?' Just at that, a big, coarse voice roared at me from the heavens. It said, 'Get out! Get out and save some souls!' With that I was back in the coffin and getting driven into Derry. The hearse pulled into the roadside. The woman said to the driver, 'Why are you stopping?' He nodded towards me in the back and said, 'He's been given a second chance.' I remember that being such a relief.

I eventually came out of the coma. As soon as I woke I had that 'dream' in my head. I couldn't speak for a couple of days. But as soon as I could speak I told my family about it. I remember it now as if it happened last night.

Somewhere in that 'dream' I had the notion that it was between me and a young girl. I thought, 'There is no chance they're going to pick me above her.' I have often wondered if a young girl died around Claudy, around that date. That's something I haven't spoken to many people about. It's a wee bit strange.

I was told, when I came around, that my family had

brought in a Padre Pio mitt on the day things improved. When the consultants eventually came around they said, 'We can't believe the changes in that man. Everything is better.' Some nurses who were in the room later told me, 'Something strange happened in the room that day.' Up to that time I was a gonner. From then on I slowly got better.

Overall I was in the hospital for nine weeks. I was in Intensive Care literally up until I came home. The first day I got up and started walking, the nurses were all out clapping. The day I left, the whole hospital was out clapping me. It was unbelievable to them. They thought, 'That man should have been dead.' The fact that I survived, and came through, amazed a lot of people.

I believe I was shown the life I was living and where I was ending up. I believe Padre Pio intervened. He went to Jesus or whoever. He said, 'There are people here praying for this man. They want him to have a second chance. Give it to him.' I believe I got a second chance, as the man said who was driving the hearse. Something definitely happened in the room that day. I will never forget it.

DOMINIC, FROM DUBLIN, experienced a vision while being resuscitated in hospital following a heart attack.

In 1996 I was on my way to work and I had a heart attack while I was driving along. Basically what happened was that I was coming onto a motorway, just beside a hospital, when I got this 'wallop' in my chest. There was no pain. It was just like a 'thump', as if somebody hit me with a concrete block. The 'thump' stayed. It was continuous. It was like an elephant sitting on my chest. I knew exactly what it was. It was a heart attack.

I said, 'My God! What am I going to do? If I go onto the

motorway, I can't stop. If I do stop, nobody will stop to help me.' I looked up and saw the hospital on my right. I couldn't believe my luck. I just drove around the roundabout and went into the grounds.

There were two people there going into the hospital. They were obviously two nurses or two medical people. I said, 'Look after me, please. My name is Dominic and I'm having a heart attack.' One took me by one arm and the other by another arm and we went in through a door into the hospital.

I was immediately in a room with a table. It was like an operating table. They put me up on this and pressed a bell. Immediately all hell broke loose. People came running from all directions, doctors and all that. They started taking off some of my clothes and hitting me on the chest. They were telling me, 'Hold on! Hold on!' That was my second heart attack and, although I didn't have any fear of dying, I probably was dying at the time.

Suddenly I looked across and saw what I can only now describe as a vision. There were three people standing in a double doorway. One was Jesus. The other was Mary. And the third was Joseph. Jesus was on the left. Joseph was in the centre. And Mary was on the right. Jesus wasn't a child or a growing youth – he was a tall man. I knew immediately who they were. There wasn't the slightest doubt in my mind.

It was totally real. The people around me seemed to disappear altogether although I knew they were there. The real people were the people standing in the doorway. They were smiling at me and greeting me and nodding their heads as if to say, 'Come in. You are very welcome.' They were in a doorway with a marble surround, like you would see maybe in the Vatican. It made me so happy. I said to myself, 'Thank heavens! I've made it! I'm alright! I'm getting in!'

There was a big space between us. From where I was on

the table over to their door was this space of about 20 feet. All I wanted to do was float across and get into this other room. I was very conscious of the big distance. I kept thinking, 'How the hell am I going to get across there?' I was annoyed with the doctors and nurses trying to bring me back and telling me, 'Hold on!' I suppose they were saying to me, 'Don't die on us!'

It was really getting on my nerves. I was terribly conscious of the fact that they were interfering with me, trying to save my life, when I wanted to cross over. So I came back to reality wanting to tell these people, 'Leave me alone! For God's sake! I want to get in over there!' But when I came back to reality I realised what was happening and that they were trying to look after me.

I looked back again at the door. Weren't the three of them still nodding but going back in and closing the double doors. They were heading away from me, back into their house. They were still facing me but going backwards. The smiles hadn't disappeared but they were just nodding like they were saying, 'It's OK. You don't want to come now. That's alright.' It was as if they were saying, 'Goodbye now.' I said to myself, 'I'm not going to die yet.' That was the end of it. Then I concentrated on what the medical people were doing. And they brought me around.

My wife and family came in to see me because, at that stage, the hospital had phoned home and said, 'You'd better come in here.' I was pleased to see them but I wasn't that upset by what happened. It seemed to buck me up a lot. I then had a quadruple bypass and, after a year or so, I got better. Both my lungs collapsed during the course of the operation so it took a lot longer for me to come back to health. But I did.

What I saw that day meant to me that despite the fact that I had been leading a normal life I must have been a little better at it than most people. Otherwise the people up above might not have been prepared to welcome me in. That's exactly what it meant. It was very much a religious experience although it didn't make me more religious or more energetic about doing my religious duties. But, looking back, it definitely was a marvellous experience, as far as I was personally concerned.

ROSE KIELY, FROM LIMERICK, was in a traffic accident back in the 1990s. She had a visitation in hospital from her deceased former boss.

On 24 November 1994 I had a serious car accident. It was a head-on collision. I was near Shannon Airport and coming back from Dublin. I was just driving along and the next minute I spotted a car a good bit down the road. I didn't really take any notice of it. The next thing he came across onto the other side of the road, facing me.

His car was bigger than mine and he was going a good speed. I knew I couldn't go left because I wouldn't have been able to get up onto the green area by the road. I knew I couldn't go right either. I knew I was dead. I said, 'That's it. I haven't a hope.' As far as I was concerned, that was it.

It all happened so fast. He kept coming towards me. It lasted probably about 30 seconds. I said goodbye to everyone. I said goodbye to my mother. My father was dead and I said, 'Dad, I'll see you shortly.' I saw my Uncle Joe. All that went through my head. I'm amazed I thought of so much. It was the loneliest time of my life.

The car hit me then. He came in on top of me. His headlights kind of came into the window at me. My roof caved in. All the windows caved in. My two knees were destroyed because they hit off the dashboard. One of my arms went into the back seat of the car. My other arm went flying out the window.

I ended up having about 20 operations on my left arm and they didn't think they could save it. I also ended up with a lot of artificial things in my hands. I'd say I could punch somebody now and knock them out because I have a lot of ball-bearings along my knuckles.

Half my hip was taken out and put into my left arm. There was blood everywhere and there was glass everywhere. I had internal bleeding. I was lucky, though, because I was wearing one of those jackets we had then that zipped up and had mock fur on the collar. I had that up covering my nose because it was very cold. I didn't have any scars on my face because of that.

I was also lucky because, although we didn't have to wear safety-belts at the time, mine was on. I had a long, tiring day and it was cold. I suppose for comfort I had put on my safety-belt. So I was lucky. But I was about three years in and out, getting treatment.

It happened just across from the fire station, which probably saved me because they got out so fast. They heard the crash. I was taken into the hospital. There were all sorts of scary things going on. In my head I thought, 'They are wasting their time on me. There's no point. They should be looking after somebody else.' I was calm and at peace because I knew I was going to die. So what was the point in all this fuss?

They transferred me to another hospital. On the first night I arrived, I slept properly. I had what I sometimes call a 'dream' but it was more than that. It was too real to be a dream. It was a beautiful day. I was sitting on rocks in Doonbeg, which I have visited only about two or three times in my life. I was sitting there on my own. They were just flat rocks, not like the rocks in Kilkee. There was a little bit of jaggedness around these really flat, spacious kinds of rocks. I was looking out to the sea.

The next thing my ex-boss, Brendan, appeared to me. He had died in a car crash years before that. He appeared to me in his suit, which he always wore – he was a 'suits man'. I looked around and he was walking towards me. I remember thinking, 'Jesus! He's still wearing his suit!' He sat down beside me and put his two hands around his knees.

It was really great to see him. He talked to me and we laughed. He said to me, 'You don't have to worry. You will just have to get better. You're not joining me yet. It's not your time.' Then he just launched into a few things that had happened in my life since he died. He started chatting about them and said, 'I'm keeping an eye on you now.'

The conversation was heart-warming. He was the sort of person who told you it as it was. He didn't flower things up. If he had bad news to tell you, he told you. He was a busy man, a straight talker. Then he just had to go. There was a kiss on the cheek and a slap on the back and he was gone.

I woke up the next day and I said, 'Right! I'd better kick on with recovery now because if Brendan says I'm not going, then I'm not going!' The impact was instant. I had the most horrendous operations after that. But, inwardly, I knew that I was going to be fine. Nothing bothered me. I was relaxed. I remember in the very last operation, my arm might have to have been removed. But I didn't care because I believed Brendan.

His wife came in to see me and I told her what happened. The word I said to her was that I had 'met' Brendan, not that it was a 'dream'. She was delighted. I also became very good friends with the surgeon I had. I told him and he was OK with it. He felt, 'Whatever gets you through!' I wouldn't be going around telling too many other people. A few people I have said it to go, 'That's mental' or 'That's weird.' But I don't care what anybody says.

I am great now. The scars have healed well although I have pins and plates in my left arm and I still go to physiotherapy occasionally. I don't think other people would look at me and know what happened. It hasn't changed me much. It's not that I believe in an afterlife. I don't, as such. I don't believe in God but I do believe in energy and the power of thought. And I do believe if you are connected to people and they go before you, they can have a certain influence on you.

What happened has definitely meant a lot to me. Although I refer to it as a 'dream', Brendan was actually with me. He was definitely there. It was more than a dream in that I felt his presence. I have tried since then and said, 'I'd love a chat, Brendan. How is it going?' But nothing has ever occurred again. Yet I know it happened back then. I know as well that I never again wish to experience the loneliness I felt that day of the crash. After what happened, maybe I won't.

FINOLA MURPHY, WHO COMES ORIGINALLY FROM COUNTY CORK **but who lives in County Dublin, had a visit from her deceased mother back in the 1980s.**

When I was at secondary school they handed out religious medals every year to the girls in each class. Every year you were a child of something. Like, one time, you were a Child of St. Joseph and you had a chain around your neck with a ribbon and a medal of St. Joseph. In your final year you became a Child of Mary, which was very big in those days, and they gave out Child of Mary medals. You wore a blue ribbon around your neck, with the medal of Our Lady hanging off it.

When they were giving them out, a friend of mine, Ruth, and I were told to leave the room because we were troublemakers, mischief-makers, and we weren't given the medal. We didn't care much. We were outside, laughing. But there was a serious side to it. It was 'smack on the wrist' at home and being told I was dreadful, terrible and disgracing the family.

I always remember that I would say to my mother, 'When I die I won't be able to be buried in the Child of Mary blue-and-white habit.' She would say to me, 'Well, I'm a Child of Mary.' We often had this discussion. Then, when I got older, it became a laugh. I'd say, 'I'm not a Child of Mary like you are.' We'd joke about it and she would laugh.

Time went on and she died very suddenly. I remember wondering would she be buried in the Child of Mary habit. Instead, when she was in the funeral home she was dressed in white, like a white shroud. Because of the trauma at the time, it never struck me to say, 'She should be buried in the Child of Mary habit.'

We stayed in her house around the time of the funeral. A few days later I came to my own home and went to bed, quite upset. It was all very traumatic. I woke up with a start in the middle of the night, maybe three in the morning. I sat up in the bed and across in the corner of the room, about eight feet up from the ground, I saw my mother. She was suddenly there. Maybe that's what woke me. And she was dressed in a pale blue, light, cloak-like gown like you'd see on a Child of Mary.

There isn't a doubt in the world but it was real. It was clearly, identifiably her. I was wide awake, sitting up in the bed and I saw her. My husband was beside me, asleep. He didn't know anything. There were no shadows, curtains or lights there, absolutely nothing. She was definitely there and I was awake. She looked alive, exactly like herself.

I saw her face and I saw her down as far as her chest. I saw the side of her face, not her full face. She wasn't facing me. I can't say her body was sideways but her head was definitely slightly turned. She was pleasant looking. She was happy and not upset. I recognised her pointed chin and white hair and everything. She was the same age as when she died. It was nearly as if she was saying to me, 'I'm fine! I'm OK!' That was the feeling I got.

I nearly collapsed when I saw her. I got a shock although I wasn't scared and it was a really pleasant feeling. It was a total surprise to me and I was transfixed. I don't know how long it lasted, maybe some seconds, but it didn't just flash in and out. She didn't say anything. Then, suddenly, she was gone. She didn't fade away. She just left.

I wondered afterwards, 'Did I dream this?' I knew I didn't. I was sitting up in the bed when I saw it. I wasn't lying down. Dreams go, they fade away, and even though you try to bring them back you can't. But this has stayed with me. To this day I can visualise it. Right now I could draw it. It was so real, as if she was in the room.

I mentioned it much later to my older brother and he said, 'That's funny, because I saw her too.' He had that experience around the same time. But we didn't really talk about it and we never got into it, which is an awful pity because we never got a chance again before he died. However, it reassured me that somebody else had experienced it.

Looking back, I'm very happy about it. I really do feel that she was telling me something. It was such a traumatic thing for her to go so suddenly and I think she came to somebody to say everything was fine. They do say that people can come back shortly after they die to let people know that they are OK. I think that's what happened.

I still feel my mother is around even now. I think all the spirits are around us, including the deceased members of my family – my parents, my brother and my nephew. People's spirits live on, probably in a different dimension. I'd like to think it is heaven but I'm not sure. But I believe my mother definitely was a spirit and was somewhere and came back. It's a memory that has stuck with me all my life.

MARIA THERESA MC CONVILLE, FROM BELFAST, was reunited with her deceased grandmother during a very complicated childbirth.

I had a bad time giving birth to my daughter back in 1993. I went 26 hours. They did everything but Constance still couldn't come out. She had a bowel movement in the womb. I was really in distress and the baby was in distress as well. I demanded a 'section'. I said, 'Get me a doctor now!' So I had an emergency section and I had to be knocked out for it.

I remember coming around in the theatre and my mum and my husband were there. They were saying to me, 'You have a wee girl.' They put me into the recovery room but they had to rush me back down to theatre because I had a haemorrhage. I haemorrhaged badly. The doctors later explained it to me as my life's blood flowing from me.

What happened next was almost like a flash of light. I had never experienced anything like it before. Everything was bright like a white light. I seemed to be at the bottom of the stairs where I lived with my mum. My granny suddenly appeared. Her name was Maria. There was a visual face on her but her body was like lights. Her body was sparkling like fairy dust. It was bright like glitter. That's the only way I can describe it. The brightness was unbelievable.

Her face was like I was looking at her in real life. It wasn't like I was looking at a ghost or a spirit. It was her. It was her face as I knew it. It was her hair as well, silvery-grey and with the wee curls she used to have. She was a wee fat lady and she had these cheeks. I could see them plainly and her colour was perfect. I could also see her hands.

I said to her, 'Granny, I want to go with you.' I reached my hand out to her. She reached her hand back to me and she said, 'No, now is not your time, go back.' I felt reassured after she spoke to me. I felt at peace. She spoke in her own voice. When she said that, I did go back and I just wakened up. The nurse then put Constance in my arms and I fed her straight away.

I believe my granny was with me. Maybe she came because she thought something was going to happen to me. I didn't really understand until a couple of days after the haemorrhage how lucky I was. That's when they told me I was very, very lucky. Yet, after I saw my granny, I got up the next morning when I wasn't supposed to. I said, 'Get me sorted, get me washed, I want out.' I was one of the quickest 'sections' that ever got out.

I feel I was being watched by my granny from a higher realm. I had been very close to her. I just idolised her. I was only 12 when she died and I was holding her hand as she passed away. We were all with her on her death-bed and she said, 'He's coming for me!' It must have been a reference to her father or one of her brothers. When I watched her die I thought, 'I'm not afraid of this.' I knew then that I wasn't afraid of death. It's one of the biggest journeys. It's like you're going into the unknown.

I believe there has to be something ahead. I'd like to think that there's a heaven, which I think is just a peaceful place. I believe it is only a veil that's separating us and I think the spirits who are there look after you and protect you. I believe you can feel them. It's like with the poem *Footprints In The Sand* – you can feel them beside you even though they are not there.

I believe the spirit lives on. A part of people never dies and I think that love never dies because you keep part of people with you in your heart. Part of them always goes on. I also believe that people come back. I believe someone always comes back to bring people over. I know my granny will probably come back to bring me over – hopefully not too soon!

ALAIN CARLIER, WHO LIVES IN COUNTY CAVAN but who is from Belgium, tells how his sister saw a vision of her deceased father.

My father, when he was alive, used to work with a pendulum and he could heal people with it. He was a farming engineer but he had very strong healing powers and he would do it as a hobby and to help people. He knew that my sister Arlette had a natural gift too. She was special. The two of them were very close. He told her that she had a gift for healing.

She realised that she could do things with her hands to heal burns. She did it at her work, if a colleague had a problem. It was working very well. For example, one of her colleagues was making coffee or tea and spilled the boiling water from the kettle on her foot. The skin was nearly coming off with the socks. But my sister put her hand on the top of the burn for maybe one minute and it was like before, all gone. So she had a lot of people coming to her.

Suddenly, in 1995 or '96, my sister had a collapse. She had a full collapse, physical and in her mind. Everything was gone, switched off. She was in her mid-50s at the time. She was not eating anymore. My mother had died around the same time, in 1995, so it was a difficult period. My sister went to hospital and she went into a kind of a coma. She stayed three months in the hospital and she was fed with liquid food.

When she was in the coma she saw my father, who had died in 1977, about 18 years earlier. He was in a kind of a blue-purple fog or light and he was coming to her. It was so real. It was not a dream. He looked not as he was when he died but as we knew him when we were young. He was saying, 'Well, Arlette, do you want to stay with us?' She didn't know what to do because she was so happy to be there that it was difficult to go back. She was surprised and she replied, 'I don't know. I'm not sure.'

She then said to him, 'It's nice here but I still have to care for my daughter. I prefer to go back.' She is a single mother and has a daughter. My father said, 'That's OK. You can go if you want.' He just faded away and she woke up. She woke up in the hospital and she didn't know where she was. She didn't know what was happening and she was very surprised.

The doctor told her after she recovered that she was using her own power and energy to heal people and that she was completely exhausted. The doctor then said to her, 'Stop everything with that kind of thing you are doing, because you can die with that.' So she stopped everything. But I still don't know how to explain what happened although there is surely some explanation.

I know that my mother was with her sister once and they saw a woman they knew, who was the landlady of the house where they were living. My mother was 8 at the time and her sister was 22 and they were coming from shopping. That was back around 1920. They saw the woman from maybe 100 yards, coming out of their own house. But she was living 60 miles away. They were thinking, 'She must be going to the station, to the train.'

When they arrived back in the house, they said to my grandmother that they had just seen the woman. My grandmother said, 'No, you must be confused because she is not well. You must have seen somebody else from another house. You are obviously wrong.' But they said, 'We are sure we saw her.' The next day they got a telegram saying that the lady was dead and she had died the morning they saw her.

I just don't know. I read a book on near-death experiences and another on recording voices from the otherworld on tapes, and there are so many different experiences. Maybe it is part of natural energy or memory or like a magnetic recording. There are so many different, special things happening. Maybe people do come back. Why not? You never know. We will know when we die, maybe.

MARIAN, FROM WATERFORD, experienced strange dreams or visions following a horrific attack back in 2006.

It was a Saturday afternoon and the sun was shining. I had only just come into the house when there was a knock on the door. This strange man was standing there. He was 6' 8" and 22 stone. I am 5' 2". He said he was looking for a B&B. I knew he had a lot of drink taken and I knew I was in trouble from the way he looked at me. I saw something in his eyes and I thought, 'Oh, my God! I'm in trouble!'

He pushed me into the hall. I got up and struggled out onto the footpath. He grabbed me under the arms and I was screaming for my life. He dragged me back into the house. He got the door closed, pushed me down and sat on me. I was lying on my right shoulder, sideways on the ground. He started thumping me into the back of the head. He kept thumping me. I was frozen with fear. In my head I thought, 'This is how I am supposed to die.'

A sort of calmness came over me. I started drifting and I knew I was going unconscious. I suddenly spoke and said, 'Oh, Sacred Heart of Jesus, please help me!' I didn't realise I was speaking the words out loud. He stopped hitting me when he heard my voice. Later I was told I was close to it but my words brought him out of his frenzy.

He said to me, 'I want money. I want a lot of money.' I led him into the sitting-room. I pulled up a venetian blind and he saw that people had gathered and were looking in. He tried to pull down the blind and, in doing so, he let me go. In the confusion I got away and I ran down to the pub on the corner. The Guards then came and arrested him and I went to the hospital and the lot.

I was very traumatised and scared after I was released from hospital. I felt terrorised and I wouldn't go out. The only way I would go from my house to the shop across the road was if I had my grandson in the pram. I felt really traumatised beyond belief. My partner had to work nights and I was so frightened that I had to go and stay in my daughter's house.

The second or third night I was there I had this 'dream' or 'vision' where dead relatives came to me. I remember getting up the next morning and saying to my daughter, 'These dead people came to me last night.' She said, 'What dead people?' I said, 'My mum and dad, Nancy my half-sister, Mary my sister, all the cousins – they were there.'

I was in a room and they were all sitting around a table with me. It was like I was holding court. All of my mother's brothers and my cousins were there. They were just like I remembered them before they died. My mum was two years dead and my dad was nine years dead. Some of my cousins had died recently. Others could be dead 30 years. The ones that were foremost were the ones that were most recently dead.

This went on for weeks. It was always the dead people. There was a lot of talking went on among them but I don't remember doing any of it. I would go down in the morning to the kitchen and say to my daughter, 'They were here again last night.' Some nights I thought, 'Oh, God! I don't want to go asleep and see all these dead people again.' I said to my daughter, 'Am I going to die? Is this why they are coming for me?' Eventually I said to her, 'They are coming to help me.' That's what I felt.

Looking back, I think my mum and dad were so horrified with what happened to me that they brought everyone I knew from the spirit world to help me and heal me. They came to me for a reason and the reason was that I was going to die from the impact of the whole thing. If I hadn't got that help I think I would have gone insane. I was just going through the motions every single day. I think, 'How would I have lived throughout all those months without the help?' They healed me every night.

I call them 'dreams' but maybe I had been visited. I don't know. They were so real. Either way, I firmly believe it was my mum put in place what happened to get me through. It was she who came to me through these 'dreams' to help me. I felt her presence. I know it was she who didn't let me die that day on the floor. I know it was she who brought me back. Whatever it was, it gave me a lift and it made me feel better every day.

What happened had a huge impact on me and has changed my whole life. I found a new spirituality. I came out of it a very different person. I have no ill feeling for that man who did what he did to me. I wasn't a church-goer but I am now. I couldn't have done all that without some superior help from somewhere else. It has brought me to the realisation that there is something greater than living.

LYNN BUFFINGTON, WHO LIVES NEAR THE CORK/LIMERICK BORDER but who comes from Delaware, USA, tells of her grandmother's death-bed experience.

My mother's mother had signed herself into a retirement village. She was an amazingly healthy woman, who never had a broken bone or anything. As time went on, however, she did lose the use of her legs. I was in university and was around 22 or 23 years of age at the time. Our exams at university ended around 19 or 20 December, just prior to Christmas, and I had come home for the Christmas vacation.

There was a note on the dining-room table from my mother, saying that she was at my grandmother's. She had received a phone call saying that my grandmother was kind of sleeping a little too much and maybe even drifting in and out of consciousness. She was also, apparently, speaking to people who weren't there.

My mother did not drive so she had somebody drop her to my grandmother's, which was a good half-hour or 40 minutes away. There was a woeful snowstorm and I thought, 'God! My mother is down there with no clothes, no toothbrush, nothing.' She had let us know she was going to spend the night. So I rang my sister and asked her would she drive there with me. She said, 'Fine.' I went and collected her. And we drove down.

My brother was a police officer at the time and he happened to be driving by the retirement home and saw my car there. It was around midnight. He said, 'Something is up.' My other brother was coming out of a card game at a bar across the road. He doesn't know what made him drive by but he did and he saw the police car and my car. He said, 'Something is happening here. I'd better go in.' So we all arrived for reasons unknown and within ten minutes of each other.

We were all standing around my grandmother's bed in her own room. We knew that she was slipping in and out of consciousness and was going to be going soon enough. One of my brothers said, 'We have to take her to hospital, she's passing away.' My mother said, 'No, it's out of the question. If she is going to go, she is going to go peacefully. We are not going to have any heroic measures, tubes or intervention, or anything.' My grandmother was 87 so what was the point.

We were all standing around, holding hands around her bed. I was holding my grandmother's hand and also my mother's. We were all entwined in a circle. Nobody was standing at the foot of the bed. We were along the sides. I think she knew she was encircled by the people that she loved.

The back of her bed was raised. She was lying there looking very attractive, with a mane of silvery hair. She looked regal. I remember watching her breathing, which was getting shallower and shallower.

Suddenly my grandmother opened her eyes. She had these vibrant, blue, piercing eyes. She literally sat up and she smiled. She looked straight ahead of her and she said, 'Oh! Jim! Tom! There you are! I can go now!' Those were her two closest brothers, who were dead long before.

She was looking straight down to the bottom of the bed, where none of us was standing. It was the most beautiful thing I have ever witnessed in my life. It was just amazing. Then she just closed her eyes and went to sleep and passed on to Jim and Tom, her two favourite brothers.

Another strange thing was that three or four of the nuns who ran the retirement home had come in and were standing behind a screen and they were singing beautiful hymns. My grandmother loved music and it felt like they were singing her home. It was the most beautiful singing ever, just what she would want.

We have talked about it since. I certainly don't believe in coincidence. I think our paths were driven there and she pulled us there. Within 15 or 20 minutes we had all arrived together. It wasn't as if we even met in the lobby. We all walked in separately to her room.

My brother was working a four o'clock to midnight shift. Had it been the previous week he would have been on the midnight to seven in the morning shift. Had my other brother not been on this card marathon until midnight he would not have been there. So it was truly amazing.

I felt blessed and I felt honoured to have been present. It was a very moving occasion. My brother cried. But I didn't cry because it really wasn't sad. It was a blessing, a celebration of her life. It was the most amazing experience I ever had and I never had it since.

I have always believed in the afterlife but if you didn't, and you had an experience like that, you would never, ever fear death. I always had a 'belief' but witnessing my grandmother gave me a 'knowing'. It was the closest I can describe to bliss. I felt all was well and my grandmother was safe home.

ANN, FROM COUNTY DUBLIN, who lost her partner through cancer, experienced a vision of him a few weeks after his death.

My partner had been sick for two years with secondary cancer. The cancer had been in remission but it came back. The primary cancer was in the kidneys and the secondary was in the lungs. There had been two prognoses – one that they could operate; the second that it was very unwise to operate because it wasn't curable and to leave it alone.

We took the decision to go for the latter and to live the rest of our lives together as best we could, enjoy ourselves and get on with it and try and put it to one side. However, after about a year it progressed and there were symptoms like breathlessness. He was on steroids and morphine.

We went to live abroad for a while because it helped his breathing. Just before Christmas he had a terrible pain in his back. He actually had a kidney infection but the pain wasn't really coming from that. Christmas was miserable because he was in terrible agony. He needed to be on a morphine pump.

Because it was easier to manage pain in Ireland, we were advised to come home. That's what we did and we came back on Stephen's Day. They found out in Dublin that he had a tumour on his spine and that's where the pain was coming from. They did radiation and shrank the tumour to some extent. But, at that stage, it was really only a matter of weeks until he died.

Within a week or two after his death, I was sleeping in the bed and I woke up. It was probably around two in the morning. I hadn't been sleeping that well because they were difficult times and I would probably wake up every night. I'd sleep for a few hours and then I'd be wide awake. But this time, when I opened my eyes, I saw him. He was standing there beside the bed. He was at the point where you pull back the blankets to get out of the bed, very close, on the left-hand side.

It was a small room so he seemed to be up at the top part of it, by the top left-hand corner. It was as if he was looking at me. I got a fright but I wasn't fearful. The room was dark but there was nothing threatening about it. Why should there have been, I suppose, because it was definitely him. I was more amazed and curious than anything else.

It wasn't a solid figure or a solid form. It was more like something you would see if you were watching a film or like an image on a television screen. But it wasn't the sort of image you would need to interpret. It was real. It was in colour. It was very clear. It was absolute. It definitely wasn't a shadow and there was nothing vague about it. There were no other shadows or anything like that in the room.

He didn't smile or say anything. He was expressionless. I didn't try to talk. And I can't remember what he wore, or anything like that, although it was probably the clothes he was normally in. But I was definitely awake and it was certainly him. He then gradually began to dissolve before my eyes. He just faded in a matter of less than a minute.

At the time there was a sense of consolation and I was glad that it happened. The feeling was a positive one and I felt it was nice. I didn't go around telling people although I did tell my family. I checked in books about it and apparently it's quite common. Only recently I mentioned it to someone whose field is psychology and she said to me it happens quite often. I also probably wished that something would happen again but it never did.

I look back on it with a feeling of curiosity although my nature is that of a sceptic. I'm not somebody who would ever have believed in the supernatural. I'm not somebody who would be going for readings with tarot cards or consulting psychics. I didn't have any firm religious conviction or beliefs. I would have even less belief in ghosts or anything like that. I wouldn't be terribly interested in that side of things and wouldn't be looking for answers there either.

It was just an experience and I don't know what it was. It's possible he came back to let me know he was OK. Maybe it's our inability to let somebody go. I can't explain it. I'm surprised that it happened and maybe there are lots of things out there that I don't understand and we don't really know about.

But I definitely know that it was real. Nobody could ever tell me that it didn't happen because I know it did. I'm 100 per cent sure of that. As to why, nobody knows although it does make me wonder.

ELIZABETH, FROM DUBLIN, lost her husband to cancer but was surprised by some visions he had shortly before he died.

My husband got prostate cancer and he had it for about five years. They put him on different things and it was absolutely marvellous. He was great for about two-and-a-half years. Eventually, however, he was beginning to have spots of blood in the urine but they'd do a little procedure and that would relieve it. No matter when he went in they would do this procedure and then he was OK again for about six months.

One time, however, he got a bad haemorrhage and he was brought into hospital in an ambulance. He was bleeding profusely. I went in the ambulance with him. We got to the hospital and they did the usual procedure. He was ready to come home and I went up to collect him. He was waiting for the doctor to come around, to discharge him.

I had the newspaper with me. He said, 'Any news in it?' I started reading out the bits he would like. The next thing I realised he was asleep. I went on reading the paper and waited. After about 20 minutes he woke up and he said to me, 'I had this very strange dream. I thought there were people around my bed, like at a wake. They were very comforting. They were very consoling.'

I said, 'Did you know any of them?' He said, 'No, but I was sorry when I woke up that they were gone.' I said to him, 'Oh, will you stop talking about wakes.' This was about two weeks before he died. Unfortunately he never left the hospital after that. He never came home.

They eventually took him down again to the theatre and the doctor did the same procedure but they couldn't stop the bleeding. They brought him back to his room after a while. They tried some new drug but after a day the same thing happened again and he started losing blood. Everything started to go awry. The doctors didn't say they weren't going to do any more but he knew it and I knew it. They took down all the tubes and everything, and both of us knew that was it.

When everyone was gone I asked him, 'Are you afraid of dying?' He said, 'Not a bit. I have come to the realisation that God loves me unconditionally.' I also said to him, 'Will you let me know if you make it?' He knew what I meant because down the years we were prayerful and I would sometimes say to him, 'If I go first, I'll let you know if there's anything there. If you go first, will you let me know?'

He used to laugh at that and say jokingly, 'If I get up there, I'll forget the whole lot of you and have a great time.' This time he said, 'I will, if he gives me permission. I'm sure I'll find some way of letting you know.'

He lived for a week and a lot happened. Lots of people came to visit. Coming towards the end I was with him and at one stage I had gone into the toilet. I think it was early morning but I'm not sure because day and night were the same to me. As I came out the door of the toilet I heard him saying out quite loud, 'It's finished. It's over. I've been through the barrier.' I said, 'What barrier?' He didn't answer that.

He was looking up at me and the two eyes were popping in his head, full of wonderment. He was all excited. He was demonstrating with his hand. If ever he was demonstrating anything, his right hand would be going up and down. He said, 'I know now what the royal priesthood means. It means we're all 'royal' because we're God's children. Nothing matters but love!'

He was shaking his hand saying it. He had such strength in his hand. He said it twice, 'Nothing matters but love!' He then said, 'If only we had the wisdom when we were young that I have now.' Then he stopped and he looked at me and he said, 'I thought I was dead. I thought I was gone.' And he started talking about God. He died the following day.

After he died I came home. I was so tired, absolutely exhausted. All I wanted to do was go to bed for a month and not have to face anything. But the following morning two neighbours came in to sympathise with me. As one of them was leaving she turned to the other and said, 'Tell her the dream you had.' She said, 'I had this dream, or whatever you would call it, and I thought I went to see your husband in hospital.

'He wasn't there but there was a bowl of rice there and I don't know what that symbolises. The dream changed and I thought I was coming out from church behind the two of you. In the distance there was blue sky and a mountain. The two of you were walking together out from the church but you got caught in a bush or wire or something.'

She then put her hands above her head, pointed to the sky and said, 'I saw your husband walking on and I saw him going into heaven.' I figure from what she told me it was the same time my husband had the experience in the hospital before he died.

It was like a bolt of lightning that went through me. I realised, at that time, that what had happened was that he was letting me know he had made it. I believe he had a look into heaven before he went. I remembered how he had said, 'I'm sure I'll find some way of letting you know.' I'll never forget the joy I felt. I thought, 'Nothing matters. He's in heaven.'

I was so full of joy that I never dropped a tear during the funeral. I never mourned him. I had no regrets about his death. I felt, 'He's in the right place.' I had nothing only a sense of wonderful joy. To this day I feel that joy. It has given me great consolation. It was the most marvellous experience and I'll never forget it.

PADDY, FROM COUNTY DUBLIN, had a sort of 'vision' of his death while ill in bed with hepatitis. He was aged 37 at the time.

I was sick with hepatitis from November through December. I was in isolation, in bed, at home. Suddenly I was at my own funeral. At one stage I was standing outside the door of my local church, watching people going into my funeral. I looked the same as I did at the time, and the same age.

The church was exactly as it is in reality – a small church, with a door that goes in almost off the street. It's only about three or four paces from the footpath to the door. I was on the left-hand side of the door, standing outside. I was there but I wasn't there, if you know what I mean. I was invisible, although it was all very real.

The weather was dry and it was winter, around November or December, that time of the year, so people had overcoats on them. The church was packed. There were people around the back. I didn't see the hearse or the coffin at all. I think the people were going in for the service and the hearse hadn't shown up at that stage. Groups of two, three and four people were filing in.

I knew everybody. I could clearly see each person but they couldn't see me. I was real but they'd just pass me by. It was work colleagues I knew and people I knew socially, not family. But they were all real people, as they were in life. My mind was very clear and I stood there ticking off a list of names in my head, saying, 'He's there. He's there. And he's there.'

The big thing that stood out for me was that, after everybody else had gone in, it struck me that there were three or four people who weren't there. They were missing. I was annoyed about that and was saying, 'Why didn't they turn up?' I felt they should have been there but they weren't. I would have known them through work and socially and they hadn't turned up. I was giving out hell at the end of it. I was very disappointed.

The other thing that upset me was that I always had a wish to go to California and I had never been there at that stage. I wanted to go there and see the Pacific and the beaches and things like that. I was very disappointed that I had died without seeing it. The sense of disappointment was huge, massive. I remember saying to myself, 'There I am. I've lived long enough but I've died without fulfilling my wish.'

I'm very sceptical about things like this, which is not to mean that I think people don't have these experiences or that they don't believe in them. I wouldn't believe in them as much as other people. I know I had a fever around the time and it could have been that, a nightmare. People who are very ill can imagine things.

But funny things can also happen to people and they can go into a different situation. I don't know. You never really know. Yet it certainly was very real and had an impact on me. Thirty years later I remember it and it's obviously been in the back of my mind. I will never forget it for the rest of my life.

SHEILA, FROM COUNTY WICKLOW, had a visitation from her deceased husband back in 2008.

My husband died in January 2000. He had been suffering for a year beforehand with complications from a bowel problem. The night before he was taken into hospital, he got out of bed and I got out of bed with him. He looked at me and said, 'Sheila, I'm dying.' I said, 'Eddie, don't talk like that.'

He had the operation and when they opened him up they couldn't do anything. He never came around after the operation. He was 18 days in Intensive Care. They had him on life-support. He was only 67 when he died and it was a big shock. I'll never get over it.

Eventually, in 2007, I had to go in for a serious operation myself. I was ill for a year before that. I was sleeping a lot, losing my balance and wasn't eating. I thought I had a tumour but I had a narrowing of the arteries caused by a problem with the spinal cord.

Then, in 2008, I had to go into hospital again to have an injection into the spine to stimulate the nerves. They're called one-shot epidurals. My arteries had narrowed and the fluid wasn't getting up into my spine and it was affecting my arms and legs. I wasn't walking too good. My right side was badly damaged. I had lost the power of my right leg and right arm.

I had the procedure and my brother picked me up from the hospital. He said, 'I think you should stay in my house because I don't want you to go home on your own.' So I stayed in his house. The following morning, around five o'clock, I was lying on my back in bed, wide awake. The door was at my back. I wasn't on medication at the time. I was on nothing. The next thing I heard my husband Eddie's voice calling me as plain as could be. He called out, 'Sheila!' It was one big shout. It was his voice. It came in through the door.

I knew the voice very well. He had a good, strong, sharp voice. In our house I had my television upstairs and he had a television downstairs because he would be looking at things that he'd want to watch and that I wouldn't be looking at. When the phone would ring downstairs he would let this unmerciful shout up to me. I had heard that shout thousands of times. It was the very same shout as if he was calling me to tell me the phone was ringing, to come down.

I'm absolutely sure it was Eddie. It was definitely him. It was exactly the same voice, the same tone, the same sharpness. His voice was as clear as if he was in the room. I'll never forget it and it was lovely to hear him. I was stunned. I said, 'That's Eddie. He's looking after me.' It was reassuring. It gave me a bit of strength.

After that I got up. My brother had said to me the night before, 'Sheila, don't get out of bed until we come down for you in the morning, because of your legs.' My walking was very bad. But, after hearing Eddie, I was able to get out of bed. I got up, went into their bathroom, got dressed and washed. When my brother came down he said, 'Oh, my God! You got up.' I said, 'Yeah, I got up and washed myself and all.' But I never told him what happened.

I said, 'Will I keep it to myself or will I tell somebody?' When you tell somebody, they look at you. People don't believe you. I did tell my daughter and she thought it was lovely. But I was slow to speak about it because I remembered back to the time when my dad died. I was very close to my mother. She'd spend a few days with me and one day she was sitting at the fire and she said, 'Sheila, I want to tell you something.' I said, 'What's wrong?' She said, 'Don't laugh and don't think I'm losing my mind.'

My mother was a nurse and was a very brainy woman. She said, 'I was in the bedroom the other night, getting ready to go to bed about half-twelve or a quarter to one. I was standing at the windows and the next thing I felt two arms on my shoulders. It was your dad. He said, "Sarah, you don't have to be worrying. I'm OK."' I asked her, 'Did you actually feel his hands?' She said, 'Yes.' I asked her, 'What happened then?' She said, 'That was it.'

Of course I was young and I laughed and I said, 'Ah, come on!' I asked her if she had told anyone else. 'No,' she said. 'You're the only one I've told.' So she didn't tell anyone either, only me. I dismissed it, to be honest, although I wouldn't dismiss it now. You know the way people are, saying, 'Is she imagining it? Is this all in her mind?' But I definitely heard the voice calling and it left an impact on me.

Looking back, I think Eddie was trying to tell me not to despair. You know the way after an operation you feel you should be able to walk and do things. You get despondent when things are not working out the way you think they should be working out. You get so angry. I think he was coming to me to reassure me. He was saying, 'Get up, Sheila! Get out of that bed and don't be lying there! Don't be depressed!'

Since then I believe in an afterlife. Strangely I've got a great calmness about dying now. I don't mind it now. I think Eddie is looking after me and hopefully we'll meet again. I often feel his presence around the house. I particularly feel his presence when I'm trying to make a big decision. I say, 'I wish Eddie was around. He'd be able to sort this one out for me.' All of a sudden I would get this lovely feeling and I would be able to make up my mind. So I feel he is around, helping me. I still feel he's there. I think he's with me all the time.

PHIL MEEKE, FROM COUNTY DOWN, describes some strange happenings that occurred around the death of his wife in 2008.

I retired from my job in 2002. We were living in the North Down direction at the time. I was working around Belfast a lot. We always wanted to build a house back down closer to Newry where my wife Jennifer grew up. We were both totally dedicated to each other, having first met at school and then getting married. I was devoted to her and she was to me. So, in 2002, I took an early retirement package and we came back down to Newry.

We built on a patch of land of one acre. It's in a rural setting and we could see the Mourne Mountains from the sitting-room. My wife loved it. Unfortunately she got breast cancer in '02, the same year as we moved. She beat it at that time, following chemo, and we were happy. But it came back five years later, in 2007, in the bones.

Out of the blue she complained of a pain in her shoulder. We got in contact with the specialist who had been seeing her twice a year. He called her in and diagnosed that it had come back. It was so aggressive it was unbelievable. They started into more chemo. She was eventually in a wheelchair. It was a devastating period for her and she suffered terribly.

She died on 28 December 2008, which was my birthday. She died at home. It was a Sunday night, at half-eight. It was her wish to die at home, in her bedroom, together with myself and our three children. She had haemorrhaged about a day before that and it broke my heart looking at it. The funeral people took her remains away and they then brought her back. We put the body in the bedroom.

On the morning of 31 December, which was the day of the burial, I was tearing myself apart at the loss. I was going in and out of the bedroom where she lay. On one occasion I walked down the corridor to the bedroom. You are talking about ten paces down the hallway, to the right. There are two windows in the bedroom, facing east to where the mountains are.

As I approached the bedroom there was this blinding light. I thought, 'That's very strange. It's only quarter to seven. The sun couldn't be up.' It was also strange to see sunlight at that time of the year.

I got one toe in through the doorway and the whole room was white. It was blindingly white. I could just about see Jennifer's face. The coffin was there on a stand and the bed had been taken out. I could see her face but I couldn't see the rest of her. Everything seemed to disappear altogether.

There was a fold-up bed there and a few chairs and some built-in wardrobes behind the door to the right as you walk in. I couldn't see them. It was as if somebody had put a couple of 500-watt halogen lights into your face.

I put my two feet into the room and the heat was incredible. It was unbelievable. It started off in my face, into my head, and I had the sensation of it going down through my body as far as my toes. I could feel it rushing down. I froze completely and I said, 'This is not normal. What's happening here?' To tell you the truth, I started to get worried about it.

I put my hand down to the radiator and touched it. I thought, 'That couldn't be on.' I knew it was off, for obvious reasons, with somebody's remains in the room. The radiator was cold. I froze for a minute or two. I kept looking. There was nothing happening. I couldn't believe it.

It lasted about two or three minutes. I couldn't move. It was so comfortable, the feeling. I felt so calm. I could think reasonably clearly but I just couldn't move. I couldn't figure it out and I was a bit scared about it. I then turned and went back up the hall.

I shouted for my daughter and she said, 'Dad, what's wrong?' I said, 'Come down. I want you to see this.' By the time we got down again to the room, the light was gone. I knew right away. I told her, 'I'm sorry but whatever it was it's not there now.' She knows that I never in my lifetime told her a lie.

It rocked me to the core, right to the centre of my bones. I've been around a few corners in my lifetime but that gave me a rocket. I don't know what it was. I can't explain it from any angle at all. I still think to myself, 'Why did I turn and walk away?' I still regret that but, obviously, there's nothing I can do now.

Jennifer was buried in our church, which is about a mile up the road. We walked behind the hearse all the way up. After the service we walked all the way back home again. That evening a second incident happened while I was carrying one of my grandchildren in my arms. He was just one year old and I was trying to occupy him. I was downstairs at the time. I decided to go up to the top of the stairs to check that no one had left the computer on in the study up there. I had heard the computer clicking or something. When I got there, the computer was off.

There is a fair-sized landing up there. I set my grandchild down. He had just started to crawl. He was looking down the stairs. I was on one knee holding his ankle as he looked down. I was thinking, 'You will not be going down there, mister, because if you hurt yourself I'll be the man in trouble.' I was immediately aware of a voice. I couldn't tell you what direction it came from. It said, in an assertive and loud tone, 'Watch that child!'

It was my wife's voice but it was in the distance. It was

definitely her. I wasn't hearing things. That's exactly what she would have said. Needless to say, I grabbed the boy and went down to the kitchen. My sister-in-law took the boy from me and told me I should sit down as my face was ashen and pale. That gave me some jolt, I can tell you.

Looking back, I regret that I didn't go further into the room to investigate the light, further understand it and deal with it. I do regret that. I also have prayed and hoped that Jennifer would speak to me again like she did that day. But she hasn't spoken to me since.

I haven't heard her voice although I have had several dreams where her two hands have been reaching out for me and her face has been close to mine. I also had a few occasions where a chair in the kitchen shifted and there was no reason for it. I wondered, 'How did that happen?'

I'm a Presbyterian and I'm a regular church-goer when I can. My wife was too. But I am also what you might call 'Mr. Sceptical'. Nothing would ever have frightened me. Yet I think about what happened every day. I wonder what it all means and I don't know. There are so many unanswered questions. I have no fear about death, none whatsoever. There has to be more – there has to be. And I just hope that wherever my wife is I can reach out and be with her again.

ETHNA, WHO COMES FROM COUNTY CORK but who lives in Dublin, was visited by her father after his death.

After my father died he used to visit me. It happened the first time maybe about three days after he died and he would visit me over about three months. The first time it happened I was in bed and was woken up by a noise like a low 'whoosh'. I think I was not going to wake up and he was letting me know he was there.

187

He appeared in the corner of the bedroom, near a window. It was the left-hand corner, as you looked out from the bed. He was up near the ceiling. He was very near me. He had jet-black hair even though his hair was grey when he died. He also looked slightly younger, about 15 or 17 years younger than when he died.

It was only his head and his shoulders, and he was dressed in a sports jacket. He was in a sort of cloud, with what was like white puffy stuff around him. The whole thing was about a foot-and-a-half square and he looked very alive. That first time it happened I got a fright and I worried about the idea of ghosts but I never got frightened after that. I used to be willing him back to speak to me.

It probably happened about six times over three months. I used to sit up in the bed and talk to him. I might get out of the bed and sit on the edge of it while I spoke. I would ask him, 'How are you feeling? Why did you leave us?' He wouldn't answer me and he never spoke to me but he would have a lovely smile on his face.

I felt he was conveying to me that he was alright. He had a tragic death, a traumatic death. I think he was letting me know that he was happy. We were all so grief-stricken that he wanted us to know he was fine.

My husband would be beside me, out cold asleep. I did wake him a couple of times. I would tell him what I was seeing and to wake up. As soon as I'd say it, my father would be gone. The last couple of times it happened, I felt he was kind of fading away from me.

There's absolutely no doubt that he was there. I am certain it happened. I suppose it was some kind of spirit. It wasn't imagination. It wasn't that I was distressed although I was upset by his death. It certainly wasn't a shadow. I am 100 per cent sure of that.

I look back on it now and, to me, it was marvellous. I still have a clear vision of it. I can still see him as plain as daylight. I tried to get it back over the years and once or twice I felt he was near me but never like that. I think he came back, at the time, because he didn't go away happy.

REDMOND ANSBRO, FROM COUNTY CORK, describes an odd experience of his mother's in 1993.

I lived with my mother at the time. She had a cottage and she lived in the front, in the cottage itself. I built an extension in the back, where I lived with my wife and three sons. One of my sons – the eldest – had his bedroom in the front of the house, next to my mother's bedroom.

On 19 December 1993 he was out with some of the lads. He came home and he heard his grandmother coughing in her bedroom. He said, 'Are you OK, Nan?' She said, 'I am.' He asked her, 'Do you want a cup of tea?' She said, 'Thanks. I will have a cup.' So he made the tea, brought it in to her and then he went to bed.

She was sitting in the bed, wide awake, having the cup of tea. We had an outside light, which was attached to a sensor unit. The next thing was the light came on. All she could see, through the window, was the outline of a man. She immediately thought it was her brother Johnny, who was a single man living in London. She couldn't make out the face. But the moment she saw the outline in the window she thought to herself, 'That's very strange, it's Johnny.' She thought he had come home for some reason.

The last time he had been home in Ireland was back in 1957. He had joined the Air Force in England in 1939 and was in the war. After the war was over, there was no word from him and she thought he had been killed. Years rolled by until she got a letter from him and he came home in '57 and stayed for three or four weeks. But he went back then and lived in Hackney in London. He never came home again although he would write to my mam seven or eight times a year. She was the closest to him.

Anyway, that night in 1993 the figure of Johnny just disappeared away from the window. My mother was waiting then for a knock on the door or for the latch to lift. But nothing happened. There wasn't a knock and no one rang the bell. After a minute or so the sensor light went off. Everything became dark again. She thought, 'It must have been someone looking for something' and she left it at that. She put it out of her mind and she went to sleep.

The following morning she walked down to our part of the house and had a cup of tea with my wife and said, 'The strangest thing happened last night.' My wife said, 'What was that?' She said, 'The light came on and I saw a figure outside the window. It moved away and I thought it would come around to the front door of the house. But there was no knock or anything.'

She said, 'The strange thing was I thought it was Johnny.' 'Johnny who?' my wife asked. 'Johnny in Hackney, in London,' she replied. My wife said, 'You must have been dreaming.' 'No,' my mother said, 'because I just had a cup of tea.' They shrugged it off and started talking about something else.

Later that day we got a phone call from London, from the Council, saying that they had found Johnny's body in his flat in Hackney. They had a contact number, because he was living on his own. Apparently he had suffered from a bleeding ulcer and it was acting up over a couple of weeks. The doctors wanted him to go into hospital to have an operation. He said, 'I won't. I will wait until after Christmas.' So he haemorrhaged and bled to death. The doctors said it had happened the night before.

We rang the Council, because they were his landlords, and they explained to us that due to the date we could forget about bringing him home until after Christmas. In the meantime, on 21 December my mother got quite sick and was moved into the Regional Hospital in Cork. While she was there, during early January, we brought Johnny's ashes home.

We went up to her and she said, 'That's great. Johnny's home and when I come out in a week or two we will have mass and we'll bury the ashes with his dad.' Unfortunately she never came out. She died on 19 January, so we had a mass and we buried the two of them together next to their father.

I honestly don't know what happened that night. My mother was very upset over it. She said, 'He called to me last night and I didn't answer.' I'm not a religious person by any means but I do believe there is something afterwards. Maybe Johnny's spirit was able to travel. I don't honestly know. Maybe he was looking for help.

My mother was clear, though. In the last month of her life she often said, 'He was outside my window the night he died.' She wasn't the sort of person to go investigating it. She just let it at that. But there was definitely something odd that happened that night.

JOHN, FROM COUNTY WATERFORD, tells how his mother died while apparently seeing a vision from the other side.

My mother was nearly 92 years old but, while she was 100 per cent mentally, her heart gave out in the end. Her body was going down a bit. She was trying to recover from pneumonia and I think the heart went on her. She wasn't particularly devout but she was a good, decent person. She attended her mass and I'd say she believed there was a God.

She was in a nursing home, in her own room. I visited her every day and would get my orders! One particular day, after tea, I dropped in to see her. I was on my way home from work. She had finished her tea and was lying there kind of asleep. When I came in she was sitting in an armchair and she had her arms stretched out as if she was about to embrace someone. It was almost like a mother would welcome a child, with her two arms raised up in welcome.

I put her two arms back inside the armchair, resting on the arm rests. She kind of stirred a little bit. She then put her two arms out again as if she was welcoming someone once more. I remember the sun was streaming in the window. I stayed with her for a while. I put her arms back in again and said, 'I'll go off now and I might come back later.'

I went home. I live about ten minutes from the nursing home. When I got in, the phone was ringing. They said, 'You had better come back out. We think your mother is dying.' I said, 'OK.' My wife said, 'I will go with you.' In the short time it took to prepare to leave – to turn off the cooker and get our coats – the phone went again. It all took less than three or four minutes. They said, 'I'm afraid she is gone.'

When we got to the nursing home they already had her in a bed, with candles beside her, and she was laid out. One of the nurses came up to me, an hour or so later, and said, 'I was with your mother at the end. She had a happy death.' She said, 'I don't know what you believe or don't believe, or whether she was hallucinating or whatever, but she put out her hands as if she was welcoming and about to embrace someone when she was dying.'

The nurse had seen it too! She wasn't a particularly young nurse and she told me she had come across it other times over the years. 'I've seen it in my career,' she said. 'Whatever the reason, your mother believed she was going to someone or welcoming someone, without question.' I wasn't surprised because I realised I had seen it myself.

I am thankful she had a pleasant death and lived to a ripe old age. I'm also thankful that she had her mind up to the time she died. As to what happened, I honestly don't know. Could it be that endorphins are released at certain traumatic times? I just don't know. But I firmly believe that at the time of death, especially in younger people, there is a consciousness that exists for a while before it dissipates. I am fully convinced of that.

I also believe that in certain people, maybe if their life-force is strong, their consciousness stays on after the moment of death. I haven't the slightest doubt about that. I also believe that consciousness can travel anywhere and can sometimes be very powerful.

As to what happened to my mum, I know it's common and I've heard people talk about it and my guess is that she believed my father was coming for her. When I was there it was like she was waiting. But there really is so much we don't know. And I don't have the answers.

UNRAVELLING THE MYSTERY

It is often said that no proof is necessary for those who believe whereas no amount of proof is ever good enough for those who don't believe at all. Such is the dilemma at the core of this chapter. No matter what evidence is presented, for or against, people will defend their long-held, entrenched viewpoints to the bitter end.

Believers – as is their right – hang onto every bit of proof, arguing that there is a heaven and that the spirit lives on after we die. They postulate that we all survive death and progress to a life hereafter. Visions and near-death journeys merely confirm their well-established positions.

Disbelievers, on the other hand, can be equally resolute, claiming – again, as is their right – that the proposition of a hereafter is nonsense and the result of wishful thinking, at best. Stories of an afterlife, they argue, are the product of psychological distress, chemical imbalances and other responses to the stresses of dying.

This chapter will attempt to steer a way through this vast chasm in perceptions. It is not an easy task, involving, as it does, a minefield of conflicting evidence, inconclusive research and diverging spiritual beliefs. Given the scale of the issue in question – the proposition that we all live on after death – things could hardly be otherwise. In the following pages I will, at least, take a stab at assessing some of the evidence.

At the core of the debate is one key conundrum – could the phantasmagorical lightshow, cornucopia of images and vivid sensory feast we experience at death have no supernatural significance but instead be the product of a dying brain? Perhaps all the bright lights, tunnels, comforting figures and visions we encounter as we die are merely a consequence of the mind going haywire and shutting down.

Alternatively, could it be that somewhere inside us all there's an evolutionary mechanism that eases our path through the trauma of death by comforting us and keeping us calm? Perhaps mankind, as it evolved, has developed a sophisticated process for reassuring those who are passing away that all is well while convincing those who live on that there will be nothing to fear when their time arrives. Mind you, if there is such a mechanism, why isn't the brain equally kind to us at other intensely-traumatic points in our lives?

Many theories have been put forward to explain the fantastic experiences that occur near death. Among them is the proposition that they are merely hallucinations caused by a restricted flow of oxygen to the brain. Brain cells require oxygen to survive and to function normally. Therefore, in the event of a heart attack or a near-drowning, for example, the brain is either partly or totally deprived of oxygen and behaves in a strange and abnormal way.

Partial oxygen deprivation is called hypoxia. Total oxygen deprivation is referred to as anoxia. In the presence of either, it is argued, a person is likely to experience light-headedness, euphoria and a tendency to hallucinate, therefore generating the sort of images recalled by interviewees in this book and elsewhere.

This theory, however, is flawed. The main problem is that entirely different sensations, such as mental turmoil, agitation and disorientation, are invariably associated with oxygen deprivation. These are far removed from the serene, peaceful feelings normally described by near-death case histories and the profound sense of calm and tranquillity they report.

In addition, while confusion and memory loss are also normally associated with oxygen deprivation, nothing of the sort is apparent in the near-death or out-of-body experience. To the contrary, the memories and images are vivid and clear and they normally remain in intricate detail with those who experience them for the rest of their lives.

Another proposition – one to quickly get out of the way – is that medication or drugs dispensed to patients during surgery, or to people who are dying, can explain the sensations or images associated with the crossover from life into death. Perhaps the most fundamental objection to this proposition is the many cases observed in all countries and cultures, including in this book, where no drugs whatsoever are involved. In addition, research has shown that, contrary to this theory, patients given painkillers or anaesthetics have fewer and less-pronounced near-death experiences.

There is one drug, however, worth examining in detail. Known as ketamine, it is an anaesthetic with a remarkable ability to produce many of the characteristics of a near-death experience. This central nervous system depressant produces psychedelic 'trips' resembling those associated with LSD. These 'trips' may be reported by patients following surgery. It is, also, not surprisingly a popular 'street' or 'club' drug in the USA.

Among the symptoms of ketamine are pleasant dream-like states, a floating sensation, experiencing a tunnel and bright light, going to another world and even communicating with a superior being. These are all remarkably similar to the near-death experience. Its role in prompting the emergence of old memories – in other words, a life review – has also been noted. Furthermore, some of those who have used the drug declare their experiences to be real.

There are, once again, some serious reservations regarding ketamine's relevance. The principal one is that those undergoing hallucinations following use of the drug often report a predominant sense of fear and paranoia. This is in sharp contrast to the near-death scenario, where reports overwhelmingly stress feelings of tranquillity and peace.

In addition, while only one in three of those who have a ketamine experience report it as being real, this contrasts with the near-death experience where people overwhelmingly describe a sense of profound reality. There is also the added difficulty, of course, in explaining cases where ketamine is not part of the treatment regime.

A further argument, popular in recent decades, is that natural chemicals known as endorphins might have a role to play. The word endorphin is a fusion of two words, endogenous and morphine. Endogenous simply means they originate from within or are naturally occurring. The word morphine is used because they reduce pain and cause pleasant sensations akin to euphoria.

These natural pain-killing substances are released by the brain at times of stress, causing a pain-free sense of bliss. They are believed to bring about 'runner's high', where people feel energetic and exhilarated towards the end of a race rather than being exhausted and in pain. They also allow soldiers to push themselves in wartime even when seriously wounded.

Perhaps then, the theory goes, a mass flood of endorphins is released in the face of imminent death, producing all the pleasant sensations that are reported in the near-death experience. Researcher Dr. Susan Blackmore concludes: 'Endorphins cause just the kinds of emotional response, including pleasure, joy, calmness and freedom from pain that occur during NDEs (near-death experiences) … It seems that the endorphins are just what we have been looking for.'

Unfortunately there are problems here as well, the biggest being that there is no proof that the brain generates a significantly greater quantity of endorphins in the face of death. Indeed, the evidence suggests that endorphins are likely to be present in equivalent amounts at other times in our lives. This has led a number of researchers to turn the question on its head and ask why we don't have near-death experiences on other occasions. Why should it only be in the face of death?

It is also pointed out that endorphins are not potent hallucinogens. In other words they are unlikely to produce the intense images and sensations witnessed in near-death journeys. It is further argued that the pain-killing properties of endorphins last much longer than the duration of a near-death experience. Thus, while there is a certain attraction to the role of endorphins in explaining some features of what we have been recounting in this book, their contribution and importance are unclear.

A further controversial theory suggests that what we experience at death is really only a mirror-image of what occurs at birth. This theory proposes that, when we die, we relive our very first birth memories including travel through a dark tunnel-like space, emergence into a light and being greeted by friendly faces such as a parent or a nurse. The proposition was first put forward by the scientist and astronomer Carl Sagan and, on the surface, it has a certain appeal.

Births happen in all cultures, to people of all creeds. The process is basically the same no matter where it occurs. Substitute a tunnel for the birth canal, emerging into the light for the birth itself, and being greeted by deceased relatives in place of parents and medical staff, and you have a readymade explanation of why near-death experiences are so remarkably similar worldwide. After all, if the death experience replicates something that is commonly shared – namely, birth – then death too will have features in common.

Once again, as with virtually all the other theories, there are serious flaws. Perhaps the most damning has followed from research undertaken by Dr. Susan Blackmore into births through Caesarean section. We would expect those who never travelled along a birth canal not to encounter tunnels in their near-death experiences. In fact, they reported tunnel travel in almost the exact same proportion to those born naturally.

Further research has also poured cold water on the theory by showing that babies really don't retain memories of their birth. One study, undertaken by Dr. Carl Becker of Southern Illinois University, concludes that babies not only don't remember being born but they also don't have the brain capacity to retain such memories. Replicating something that cannot be recognised or recalled is obviously a non-starter.

Another negative is that the experiences of birth and death, although superficially similar, are really fundamentally unalike. Dr. Raymond Moody, for instance, suggests that the birth experience isn't quite as wonderful as we might like to believe. Not only does it involve great disruption to an unborn child's universe but babies are 'pushed out into a world where they are turned upside down, spanked, and cut with scissors to sever the umbilical cord.' These are not quite the calm, peaceful journeys reported by those who are dying.

Before moving on to the out-of-body experience, it is worth mentioning another potential banana skin for proponents of the afterlife – the question as to why people from diverse cultures and religions report different elements in their near-death experiences. Although those who support the 'afterlife' theory argue that the core experience is commonly shared, the evidence is conflicting, to say the least. Not only do the superficial manifestations differ between varying cultures and religious affiliations but some aspects of the fundamental experience can differ too.

Christians may report meeting 'Jesus' or 'Mary' while Hindus meet Gods like 'Vishnu' and 'Shiva'. Christians speak of arriving at 'Heaven' while Moslems visit 'Paradise'. Christians relate how they were told to return because 'the time isn't right' while Hindus are often sent back because of a 'clerical error' caused by assistants to the God known as Chitragupta, who keeps records of people's lives and decides where they go when they die. Surely, critics argue, the afterlife should be the same for one and all – unless, of course, the images are fantasies rooted in our differing cultures and creeds.

Research certainly reveals some very notable disparities. Comparing studies from throughout the world we can see that only two features of the near-death experience are commonly shared – the concept of 'entering another world' and the 'meeting with other beings'. The 'out-of-body' experience is shared by some. This, critics argue, is hardly earth-shattering evidence of a commonly-shared fundamental experience, especially when features such as 'travel through a tunnel' and 'witnessing a light' are missing from non-Western reports.

Why, we might ask, should this be the case? For a start, culture and religion most certainly have a role to play in explaining the phenomenon. It was interesting to note, during the writing of this book, just how many people spoke of encountering some sort of ethereal and indescribable 'superior being' but couldn't, at the time of the experience, identify who it was. It was only later that some interpreted the images as

'Jesus' or 'Mary' or the 'Divine Mercy', having thought about it and sought for a way to explain it to others.

Their descriptions were, of course, rooted in the culture or creed to which they belonged. Even self-proclaimed atheists sometimes reached for images associated with the religious affiliations of their youth or the popular icons of established faiths. No surprise, then, that those from differing cultures might explain a near-death experience or vision using imagery or language understandable to their friends and acquaintances.

Perhaps, also, people from different cultures emphasise certain specific elements of the experience while excluding others. For example, it was not uncommon in my research – although this was mostly rooted in Ireland – for case histories to be uninterested in, or even dismissive of, one or two elements of the experience yet to be enthralled by others which they vividly described. It just might be the case that tunnel travel and witnessing bright lights don't rate in certain cultures quite like a meeting with lost relatives or a 'superior being'.

When it comes to the out-of-body experience the evidence is similarly inconclusive although thought-provoking, to say the least. Some argue that the phenomenon is no more than a dream, reflecting the images and emotions almost all of us experience during sleep. It is said that a specific form of dreaming is involved – known as lucid dreaming – where the dreams appear to be real, the dreamers are aware they are occurring and they can actively play a role in influencing the outcome.

There are, however, many problems with this explanation. Perhaps the most damaging derives from the circumstances under which dreams occur. Rapid Eye Movement (REM) sleep is the fifth, and final, stage of sleep, which most people experience each night. Our eyes dart around rapidly. We have elevated pulse rates and our brain activity is intense. Our muscles are, in effect, paralysed and we lose our reflexes. It is also the time when we dream.

In sharp contrast, studies clearly show that out-of-body experiences are unconnected to REM sleep. Indeed, as we have seen earlier in this book, most people leave their bodies during an awakened state and not during sleep. The examples we have encountered include people who left their bodies immediately following a car crash, a near-drowning, an acute haemorrhage, a heart attack or other traumatic events, when the issue of sleep – and, even more so, REM sleep – doesn't arise.

Further differences between dreams and out-of-body states are also glaringly apparent. For a start, those who travel outside their bodies are convinced they have separated from their physical form. On the other hand, those who dream normally remain within their physical selves and are sure the dream is exactly that – a 'dream' – no matter how vivid or lucid the experience might be.

In addition, dreams are seldom recalled with the same intensity as out-of-body experiences, where crystal-clear recollections of precisely what occurred are retained for life. Even in the case of vivid, dramatic dreams, our memories of the fine details fade or disappear over time. What we recall tends to change and evolve. An out-of-body journey, on the other hand, is remembered in unchanging detail. The impact on a person is also far more profound.

A further proposition put forward is that the out-of-body experience may be a form of what psychologists refer to as dissociation or depersonalisation. This state of mind is common. For example, a driver might not be able to recall the details of part of a car journey. He may have, for a time, dissociated himself from the task at hand. He might say he was 'elsewhere'. Other times people may daydream, or dissociate, while looking out a window or at the sky. There are further more serious examples, as a contributor to this book, psychologist Michael Paterson, outlines.

'It could happen as a result of trauma,' Paterson explains. 'For example, where there's been prolonged childhood trauma more severe cases of dissociation often occur. If you can imagine a little girl who hears footsteps on the stairs, the door opens, the light from the landing comes in, and somebody comes into the room and sexually abuses her. It is painful, it hurts her and it is emotionally disturbing to her.

'The next night there are footsteps on the stairs, the door opens, the light comes in, somebody comes in and starts to abuse her, and she focuses on a poster of Cinderella's castle. The next night the abuser comes in and, just as she's touched, she again goes into Cinderella's castle. The next time again, whenever the door opens and the light comes in, she's already in Cinderella's castle.

'That's how she learns to deal with life's stress. That's her way of coping. So, whenever she's in a stressful situation from then on, she moves in this dissociated state almost as if she is in Cinderella's castle watching a little girl being abused, separate from her body.'

Although appealing, the dissociation theory also has limitations in explaining what goes on. How, for example, can it account for those who journey out of their bodies and gather information that is only accessible at another location some distance away? How did Mary Kenny, in an earlier chapter, become aware of a dead body, and its identity, in the hospital mortuary away from where she had just given birth? Perhaps telepathy, imagination, coincidence or chance are involved. Or maybe not, as the following research studies indicate.

The best-known study in this regard was conducted by a Californian parapsychologist, Dr. Charles Tart, who undertook a series of tests with a woman who could spontaneously trigger out-of-body experiences. The aim of the tests, which were run under laboratory conditions, was that the woman would leave her body and read a five-digit number written on a small piece of paper placed on a high shelf, out of her range of sight.

The tests were conducted over four nights. On the first night she never left her body. On the second night she had an out-of-body experience but failed to float high enough to see the paper. On the third night she again left her body but travelled outside the laboratory and made no effort to read the paper. On the fourth night, however, she did read the piece of paper and correctly reported the number as '25132'. The odds of this happening by chance were assessed as one in 100,000.

In a separate study, Dr. Karlis Osis, Director of Research at the American Society for Psychical Research, tested a volunteer's ability to identify objects during a series of out-of-body experiences. The volunteer – artist and author, Ingo Swann – was asked to draw all of the objects he could identify in a box suspended two feet beneath the high-ceilinged experiment chamber.

The objects were positioned so that they would look distinctly different when viewed from a range of perspectives. Swann was then attached to a machine, located in an adjoining room, to test brain waves, heart rate, respiration and other bodily signs. He could barely move such was the tightness of the cables and other restraints. Following the experiment he was asked to provide both verbal descriptions of what he had seen and a series of sketches.

The results, which were carefully evaluated by an independent psychologist, produced a match for eight out of eight observations in a row. The odds of this happening by chance were estimated as one in 40,000. Further experiments undertaken with Swann were less conclusive although he was able to identify items such as a letter opener, including its colour, and also a small golden cross strung on a safety pin – all described from angles consistent with being outside his body and up close to the objects.

A third famous test involved a young university student and future parapsychologist, Keith Harary, who was asked to leave his body and travel to a room containing one of his pet kittens. Harary – known as 'Blue' to his friends – located himself in a room at the Duke University campus in North Carolina, USA. The kitten was kept in a laboratory some distance away. The plan was for Harary to leave his body at times selected randomly by computer while the kitten would be simultaneously monitored for any changes in its behaviour.

The results were remarkable. The kitten – named Spirit – was described by one of the organisers as 'energy-charged' and was known to scamper about on the platform which had been specially designed for the test. However, during the periods when Harary was prompted to visit the cat, the animal was calm, hardly moved at all and stopped meowing. The pattern was so noticeable that observers at the test could clearly pinpoint the times when Harary was present.

Turning to the issue of visions or visitations, an explanation is frequently put forward similar to that proposed for the out-of-body experience – namely, that they are nothing more than dreams. It is often noted, and indeed seen in an earlier chapter, that many of these dramatic events occur at the edge of sleep. Although unarguably vivid and real, they may, some experts say, be more accurately associated with illusions, hallucinations and anomalies of perception than with genuine visits from the land of the dead.

This argument, at first, seems convincing particularly when we consider what can occur as we enter or emerge from sleep. When we are falling asleep or waking up, strange things can happen. At either of these two stages, the mind is neither awake nor asleep. It is, instead, resting in a 'floating' state. Experts point out that, at both stages, images stored deep in our minds can merge with the real world in the oddest of ways.

We might, for example, bring up an image of a deceased relative and merge it with a damp patch on the wall of a bedroom. We might, instead, fuse it with the shadows cast by a curtain. In either case, vague and ethereal shapes may appear as if from the otherworld. Add in a fantasy-prone personality, or someone distressed from a recent bereavement, and the potential for replacing reality with imagination is readily apparent.

This thesis, of course, would be instantly undermined if information was imparted during the vision or visitation that could not have been known to the recipient before the event had taken place. A classic example, illustrating precisely this, exists. The story was chronicled by the eminent physicist, Sir William Barrett, back in the 1920s, a decade-and-a-half after his tenure as professor at Dublin's Royal College of Science came to a close.

The case, involving a woman who was dying from heart failure following the delivery of her child, was witnessed by Barrett's wife – the obstetric surgeon Lady Barrett – and also by the hospital's resident medical officer, the matron and the dying woman's mother. 'Oh, lovely, lovely,' the dying woman unexpectedly exclaimed on her death-bed. 'What is lovely?' Lady Barrett, who delivered the child, queried. 'What I see,' the woman replied in low intense tones. 'What do you see?' Barrett asked. 'Lovely brightness, wonderful beings,' she responded.

Focusing her attention intently on one particular spot in the room, she exclaimed, 'Why, it's Father! Oh, he's so glad I'm coming; he is so glad.' She continued, 'I can see Father; he wants me, he is so lonely. I am coming.' She added, 'Oh, he is so near.' Then, with a rather puzzled expression, she exclaimed to her mother, 'He has Vida with him.' Staring directly at her mother, she repeated in astonishment, 'Vida is with him.'

Vida was the dying woman's sister who had passed away more than two weeks earlier. The woman, however, had not been informed of this tragic development. Instead, the family had acceded to a request from the matron and carefully withheld the information due to the seriousness of the patient's condition. Even letters were censored, as her mother later confirmed in written testimony.

'All her letters were also kept by request until her husband had seen who they might be from before letting her see them,' the mother wrote. 'This precaution was taken lest outside friends might possibly allude to the recent bereavement in writing to her, unaware of the very dangerous state of her health.'

For the record, the unfortunate young woman – referred to in Barrett's book *Death-Bed Visions* as 'Mrs. B.' although we know her first name was Doris – died on 12 January 1924, two weeks and four days after the death of her sister Vida, who departed the world on Christmas Day 1923. Their deaths brought to a conclusion one of the most perplexing –

and, for afterlife proponents, significant – death-bed visions in history.

The possibility that chance played a role in the case was summarily dismissed by Barrett. Had it been a one-off event, he argued, the case for coincidence might be credibly sustained. 'If this case stood alone this would be the probable explanation,' he conceded. There were, however, so many other cases he had come across that 'mere chance coincidence cannot apply.'

Barrett likewise stressed how so many of the subjects he studied, including the tragic woman, had been lucid and rational at the time of the visions. He further emphasised how preconditioning appeared to have no role to play, pointing specifically to cases he encountered of dying children who insisted that angels they had seen were wingless and, to use one child's words, 'they just come' but 'don't fly', contrary to the well-established perception at the time.

Almost four decades later, Dr. Karlis Osis – the para-psychologist we heard of earlier in this chapter – confirmed Barrett's findings in an American study of his own. Osis once again established that people on the verge of death may be greeted by welcoming figures, most notably deceased family or friends. He also observed that medication was not a contributory factor; nor were the people delirious or hallucinating. He further concluded that many of the patients knew these figures were coming to take them to the other side.

The Osis study additionally established that even terminally-ill patients, who knew of their pending demise, mostly witnessed the visions close to the point of death. It would appear, the study inferred, that it is primarily in the hour or so before dying that comforting figures visit those about to cross over. The outcome of Otis's study seemed to echo the conclusion drawn by Barrett back in the 1920s: 'These cases form, perhaps, one of the most cogent arguments for survival after death.'

So where does this leave us in the quest for establishing what, if anything, happens after we die. Which argument does the evidence support? The research, unfortunately, is inconclusive, contradictory and sometimes speculative, to say the least. While no single theory fits, some experts – the most prominent being Dr. Susan Blackmore – argue that a combination of elements, including oxygen deprivation and endorphins, among other factors, may hold the key. Others believe that a more fundamental explanation will eventually be found.

Some believe the answer lies in what are called the temporal lobes of the brain. There are two of these lobes – one at the right, above the ear; the other similarly located on the left. Studies have shown that a particular type of epilepsy known as temporal lobe epilepsy can produce a life review and sensations similar to floating outside the body as well as dream-like states and religious sensations. Perhaps then, it is argued, something similar happens in the face of death whereby the same type of activity is triggered in our temporal lobes.

There are, as with all theories examined so far, limitations to this proposition. For a start, the common emotions linked to epileptic seizures include sadness, fear and loneliness whereas near-death experiences involve joy and intense feelings of peace and calm. Researcher Dr. Michael Sabom additionally concluded that the life reviews associated with seizures involve only one single event whereas multiple images, occurring in rapid succession, are associated with the near-death experience. The temporal lobe theory, although still popular with some researchers, is another non-runner, Sabon concluded.

My own view, from the evidence I have encountered, is that somehow, in some shape or form, life does continue after death. Whether that entails the survival of our mind or our consciousness separate from our physical form, or the departure of our 'spirit' or our 'soul' to another world, is not clear. What is apparent, though, from those I interviewed for this book, is that the moment of clinical death, when our heart has stopped beating and our brain has flatlined, is not the end of the story.

Which brings us full circle; back to those early Irish churchmen, Fursa and Adamnán, and to the reprobate Tundale, who were discussed at the start of this book. Back to even earlier times, when our forebears were first formulating their views of the otherworld and what happens when we die. Back to an era that predates even Abraham, Isaac and Jacob, when our predecessors struggled to lift the veil on what awaits us after death.

We can imagine the scene, with our early ancestors enthralled by the extraordinary tales of tunnels, bright lights and a 'superior being' recounted by those who undertook the first near-death and out-of-body journeys. Those early stories, with their vivid afterlife images, found their way into the core manuscripts of various faiths. Where else did the first concepts of heaven originate than in narratives identical to those being reported today?

Not surprisingly, the imagery in ancient texts is remarkably familiar. In the Book of Ezekiel we hear how the prophet Ezekiel was transported to heaven, where – just as with interviewees in this book – he encountered 'a likeness as it were of a human form' surrounded by light of intense brightness. Similarly, in what could be a reference to the life review and the light at the end of the tunnel, John 3:20 tells us, 'Everyone who does evil hates the light, and does not come to the light lest his deeds should be exposed.'

The images surrounding Jesus are equally familiar. Describing himself as 'the light of the world' Jesus proclaimed, 'Whoever follows me will never walk in darkness, but will have the light of life.' He also spoke of coming into the world as 'a light, so that no one who believes in me should stay in darkness.' Psalm 27:1 says, 'The Lord is my light and my salvation; whom shall I fear?'

St. Paul, it is now believed, almost certainly had a near-death experience on the road to Damascus. He was, the Bible tells us, approaching Damascus when 'suddenly a light from heaven flashed about him.' The saint, in his later writings, described how he had been 'caught up into paradise' and was confused about how it had occurred – 'whether in the body or out of the body I do not know.'

In the Islamic tradition, Muhammad had his vision while enveloped by an angelic presence and with his soul 'being torn away' – a phrase reminiscent of a near-death experience. In Hinduism, the sacred Sanskrit scripture known as the Bhagavad Gita describes one of the roads travelled by souls after death as 'the path of the sun.'

Perhaps, then, our many religions are grounded more in natural experiences and less in the supernatural than we have been led to believe. Many now argue that the fundamental truths they once espoused – truths inspired by the experiences of those who had travelled, however briefly, to the borders of death – have somehow been lost over time. An insightful ancient parable related by Mally Cox-Chapman in her book *The Case For Heaven* sums up the point quite well.

An isolated natural spring, she recounts, once existed in a desert. Thirsty travellers would stop there to drink. Each traveller placed a stone at the spot to help identify the well's location, which was particularly hard to find. The stone also marked their visit. The routine became a tradition.

Unfortunately the well was soon covered over with stones and the water could no longer be seen. The sound of the water, however, was still clearly audible. Travellers therefore continued to deposit stones, listening to the gurgling of the spring, until eventually even the noise disappeared.

In time, with both the sight and sound of the water lost to history, travellers could no longer remember the reason why a heap of rocks lay in a pile in the desert. People had forgotten the purpose of why they put stones there. Yet they still did it. It was, after all, a tradition!

Like the parable – and like religion – perhaps we, too, have lost touch with the fundamental principles of an afterlife which were widely known to our forebears and which provided unique insights into life after death. For a time, long ago, they were the bedrock of our faith, the foundation of our beliefs and the template for a happy death and a path to the afterlife. Then they were lost to history.

Having been dusted off, re-examined and reassessed, no one doubts – not even the sceptics – that near-death experiences are real and do happen. What's more, although their cause and consequence are unclear, they are likely to be what faces us at death – joyous and happy journeys, replete with warm, peaceful feelings and a reunion with those we once loved, in the company of a being often referred to as 'God'. Whether that means eternal life – well, the jury on that one is still out!

ACKNOWLEDGEMENTS

This book would never have happened without the many so-called ordinary people who stepped forward to tell their extraordinary stories. Covering all four provinces and the majority of counties, they related their narratives with sincerity and an extraordinary attention to detail, despite reliving what can only be described as intensely emotional and traumatic life events. I can never thank them enough.

Some of those I interviewed wished to remain anonymous while others requested first names only. These conditions I agreed to although the use of false names was never permitted. Not everyone's accounts are included due to pressures of space. I apologise for any disappointment I might have caused. I would also like to thank all those who sent articles, clippings and messages of goodwill. Their thoughtfulness is much appreciated.

Many newspaper editors responded to my pleas for help, among them the editors of the *Belfast Telegraph*, *Kerryman*, *Limerick Post*, *Irish Catholic*, *Ireland's Own*, *Western People*, *Munster Express*, *Connacht Tribune*, *Southern Star* and *Waterford Today*. The appeals they published on my behalf produced an outstanding response, for which I am grateful. I would also like to single out the editor of the *Wexford People*, who gave permission to quote passages from a feature report.

On the book front, Dr. Raymond Moody's groundbreaking *Life After Life* and *The Light Beyond* were indispensible reading. Other helpful titles included *Closer To The Light* by

Dr. Melvin Morse, *Lessons From The Light* by Dr. Kenneth Ring and Evelyn Valarino, and *The Near-Death Experience: Problems, Prospects, Perspectives* by Dr. Bruce Greyson and C. P. Flynn.

Also helpful were *Beyond The Light* by P. M. H. Atwater, *The Return From Silence* by D. Scott Rogo, and *The Case For Heaven* by Mally Cox-Chapman. Although all the above works are predominantly rooted in the USA, they offer a familiar framework within which the Irish experience can be assessed and understood.

Among the British books I would recommend are *The Truth In The Light* by Dr. Peter Fenwick and Elizabeth Fenwick, *Beyond The Body* and *Dying To Live* by Dr. Susan Blackmore, *Death's Door* by Jean Ritchie, and *I Remember Dying* by Paul Roland. Another British book, *The Afterlife* by Jenny Randles and Peter Hough, provides an interesting overview of the mysteries surrounding life after death, including a chapter on the near-death experience.

Other texts include P. M. H. Atwater's comprehensive and eminently-readable *The Big Book Of Near-Death Experiences* and Anthony Peake's brilliant *Is There Life After Death?* Be aware, though, that Peake's work, although outstanding and genuinely life-changing, is very tough going. There are also many books detailing personal testimonies, perhaps the best known being Betty J. Eadie's *Embraced By The Light*.

Much of the early groundbreaking work in Ireland, in terms of collecting and publishing real-life stories, was undertaken by Sir William Barrett, who worked as Professor of Physics at the Royal College of Science in Dublin from 1873 – 1910. Barrett was one of the great investigators of the spiritual world and one of the first chroniclers of the near-death experience. His excellent *Death-Bed Visions* was published in 1926, shortly after his death. His other works include *Psychical Research* and *On The Threshold Of The Unseen*.

Further studies were conducted by the eminent Church of Ireland archdeacon, St. John Drelincourt Seymour, who lived in County Tipperary. This prolific author, who published in the early decades of the twentieth century, was responsible for titles including *Irish Visions Of The Other World*, *Irish Witchcraft And Demonology* and his seminal *True Irish Ghost Stories*. Although his works are fascinating in their own right, they had only marginal relevance to the theme of this book.

Finally, regarding books, there are many translations of the ancient experiences of Fursa and Adamnán and the medieval tales of Tundale. For a broad exposition of their stories I would strongly recommend *Visions Of Heaven And Hell Before Dante* by Eileen Gardiner. Another interesting work is *Otherworld Journeys* by Carol Zaleski.

Many individuals were also of immense assistance and deserve credit. My thanks to journalist Gráinne McCarry, from Northern Ireland, who helped identify some excellent interviewees. Jerry O'Sullivan was ever-helpful in Munster. Kay Healy was a willing source of contacts in County Wicklow. Also invaluable was Finola Murphy, who identified case histories in various parts of the country and read the text.

My special thanks to Linda Monahan of Typeform for her general helpfulness and her skill in designing the cover. Typeform's Roy Thewlis was always accommodating, as was Pat Conneely who laid out the text with his usual professional care. My appreciation also goes to the staff at ColourBooks, especially David O'Neill.

My gratitude to Colum Kenny, whose conversations with me helped formulate the original shape of this book and who brought me interesting reading material back from the USA. Kathleen O'Connor was generous with her insights, as always. Others deserving thanks include Ben from County Galway, G. Quinn from County Roscommon, and Richard T. Cooke from Cork, who will each know why they are mentioned.

Finally I would like to thank Úna O'Hagan who was involved right from the start of this project. There are few aspects of the book where her presence wasn't felt, including devising the format, shaping the chapters, deciding on the cover and title, and proofing and reading the text. Her role was invaluable in bringing such a complicated and often intense project out of the darkness and into the light.